Mastering Swift Package Manager

Build and Test Modular Apps Using Xcode

Avi Tsadok

Apress®

Mastering Swift Package Manager: Build and Test Modular
Apps Using Xcode

Avi Tsadok
Tel Mond, Israel

ISBN-13 (pbk): 978-1-4842-7048-6   ISBN-13 (electronic): 978-1-4842-7049-3
https://doi.org/10.1007/978-1-4842-7049-3

Copyright © 2021 by Avi Tsadok

Managing Director, Apress Media LLC: Welmoed Spahr
Acquisitions Editor: Aaron Black
Development Editor: James Markham
Coordinating Editor: Jessica Vakili

Distributed to the book trade worldwide by Springer Science+Business Media New York, 1 NY Plaza, New York, NY 10004. Phone 1-800-SPRINGER, fax (201) 348-4505, e-mail orders-ny@ springer-sbm.com, or visit www.springeronline.com. Apress Media, LLC is a California LLC and the sole member (owner) is Springer Science + Business Media Finance Inc (SSBM Finance Inc). SSBM Finance Inc is a **Delaware** corporation.

For information on translations, please e-mail booktranslations@springernature.com; for reprint, paperback, or audio rights, please e-mail bookpermissions@springernature.com.

Apress titles may be purchased in bulk for academic, corporate, or promotional use. eBook versions and licenses are also available for most titles. For more information, reference our Print and eBook Bulk Sales web page at http://www.apress.com/bulk-sales.

Any source code or other supplementary material referenced by the author in this book is available to readers on GitHub via the book's product page, located at www.apress.com/978-1-4842-7048-6. For more detailed information, please visit http://www.apress.com/source-code.

Printed on acid-free paper

Table of Contents

About the Author

Avi Tsadok is an accomplished iOS developer with almost a decade of experience. He currently heads mobile development at Any.do, a leading productivity app. He's also a regular contributor to *Better Programming* and has an active presence on Medium. He uses writing to combine his passion for helping educate the development community while working on refining his own skills in developing.

About the Technical Reviewer

Felipe Laso is a senior systems engineer working at Lextech Global Services. He's also an aspiring game designer/programmer. You can follow him on Twitter at @iFeliLM or on his blog.

CHAPTER 1

Introduction

Programming without an overall architecture or design in mind is like exploring a cave with only a flashlight: You don't know where you've been, you don't know where you're going, and you don't know quite where you are.

—Danny Thorpe

If you are reading this book, you are probably an iOS developer already. This is not a book for beginners or developers who never touched Xcode in their lives.

And if you did build an app or two, you already worked with frameworks and modules.

In fact, you are using frameworks and libraries every day, even if you are not aware of them.

Foundation, UIKit, Core Data, SwiftUI, StoreKit, and many more are just a few examples of frameworks we use every day.

Apple has over 120 frameworks and libraries in their SDK, and this number is growing with every iOS version released.

Frameworks and libraries are a great way to share and bundle different technologies or services.

Sometimes, when talking about third-party services, it's the main and only way to do that.

But frameworks/libraries/modules are not just for Apple to provide us development tools or for companies to share their API with us.

© Avi Tsadok 2021
A. Tsadok, *Mastering Swift Package Manager*,
https://doi.org/10.1007/978-1-4842-7049-3_1

We, as developers, can make use of libraries in our apps and projects.

Separating our apps into modules gives us a different aspect of how projects are built and the internal relationships between them.

Personal View

Implementing Swift Packages in my projects was a personal revolution I had in my development career.

The technical details on how to do that are not important – you can find them in every blog, manual, or Apple developer website.

But instead of looking at my project as an extensive set of classes with unclear relationships, I started to look at it as a group of technologies with clear responsibilities and a defined API.

Each module can be shared, tested, and improved over time.

And for me, it wasn't just a minor change – it was a giant leap forward.

My project improved in every level – it was more stable, more testable, and even faster.

It's not that Swift Packages have a secret feature that makes your project run better.

The process of creating a Swift Package forces you to take good and healthy steps that eventually improve your projects, such as testing, API design, dependency injection, documentation writing, and many more.

Once I did that, I realized how important it is to modularize my code, be organized, and work with "API-driven" design.

The Future by Apple

Building modular apps was always possible in iOS and macOS. We have frameworks and static and dynamic libraries. But in the end, the key is **how you manage your dependencies** efficiently.

Over the years, Apple focused on driving the MVC pattern forward.

But in the last 2–3 years, things have changed, and we can see the new direction Apple is taking us:

SwiftUI – SwiftUI is Apple's declarative framework for building user interfaces, based on some Swift language features and ideas taken from other declarative frameworks such as React and Flutter.

With SwiftUI, Apple is, in fact, dumping MVC. So, what is the new design pattern that we're using here? We don't have a controller, but we know we have a view and a model. The view is binding to the model through an observable object which acts as a view model. As a result, we can say that the classic SwiftUI implementation is much like MVVM.

What's also interesting is that SwiftUI is how Apple wants us to build in **all of its platforms**, not only iOS.

For Apple, SwiftUI is the future.

Swift Package Manager – When Apple introduced Swift Package Manager, we could create a new Swift Package using the command line only. But starting Xcode 11, creating a new Swift Package is built into Xcode, including dependency configuration. We see further improvements in Xcode 12 that allow us to add resources and files to a package and make it much more powerful, almost like a complete framework.

We can conclude that Apple sees Swift Packages as the basic logic unit of all of our apps.

Combine – Once we have a declarative UI framework (SwiftUI) on the one hand, and on the other hand a set of libraries, it is just natural to manage the data flow with *Combine*. Combine is Apple's version for RxSwift, a reactive framework that can help you handle process values over time, and it was introduced along with SwiftUI in WWDC 2019.

It is the glue that connects the business logic to the UI layer.

So, if we put it all together, we'll see something like Figure 1-1.

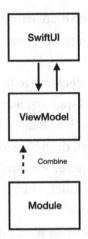

Figure 1-1. *How Combine, SwiftUI, and Packages go together*

If we want our projects to fit in with how Apple sees the future of development, we now understand that Swift Packages play a significant role and how important it is to start and change our mindset on how our apps are built.

About This Book

This book is not a manual or documentation.

I was so excited about Swift Package's changes to my projects, so I wanted to explore that area even more profoundly – what it means about architecture, code coupling, API design, and more.

And while I was scratching more and more layers, I realized that the thing called "Swift Package Manager" is much more than a technical project component – it's a whole new perspective.

You will find here how to create and maintain Swift Packages both from Xcode and Terminal, at the deepest level possible, and how to do it **right**. And this is what this book is all about.

Even though you can read this book in whatever order you wish, reading it chronologically is the recommended way to go – from theory and design to basic Swift Package maintenance, distributing, and finishing with testing and resources management.

Throughout the book, you will meet the iOS development team of "Weathery Apps" – an imaginary company that struggles to improve their app using Swift Package Manager for the first time.

In each chapter, the team encounters a real-world problem and solves it using different Swift Package Manager features or aspects that will be widely discussed.

Enjoy the reading!

CHAPTER 2

Organized Mess

Every program attempts to expand until it can read mail. Those programs which cannot so expand are replaced by ones which can.

—Jamie Zawinski

Before we run forward and talk about Swift Packages, frameworks, and libraries, we need to prepare our app for that.

In the bottom line, packages are just another technical expression of good architecture and reusable code. It is almost inevitable to organize your project if you want to implement Swift Packages.

In this chapter, you will

- **Meet "Weathery,"** an imaginary project that we follow in this book

- Learn what the **separation of concerns** principle is when talking about architecture

- Learn what the three-layer architecture is and what its benefits are

- Understand how to **redesign our app** by using a UML

- Learn what closed/opened layers, design patterns, entities, and interfaces are

© Avi Tsadok 2021
A. Tsadok, *Mastering Swift Package Manager*,
https://doi.org/10.1007/978-1-4842-7049-3_2

Meet "Weathery"

It was a lovely day at "Weather Apps," the company behind "Weathery," the App Store's best weather app.

"Weathery" is a long-existing app and has millions of downloads.

Even though a weather app sounds like a small project, it has a varied list of features, such as

- *Authentication flow, with registration, login, and forgot password feature*

- *A search engine*

- *Location-aware features*

- *In-app purchase*

- *Beautiful screens that show weather in various places in the world*

- *A user configuration page*

- *Analytics*

Other than that, the "Weathery" iOS team is adding more features and bug fixes daily, trying to keep the app stable and agile and keep pace with its competitors.

"Emily, can you come for a second? I need to talk with you about the direction we want to take" – a sound was heard in the open space out of the VP Product mouth.

Emily was the iOS tech lead of the app for the last 3 years. She knew every single line of code and was in charge of the most advanced features the app has.

"We see an increased demand for an Apple Watch version. Many users ask for that. We want to take the current version and build a dedicated Apple Watch version. The plan is to do the same for macOS in the future, but as I said, we want to start with the Watch first. What do you say? How easy is it? We already have the logic written, don't we?"

The Weathery Project

To understand if Emily can try to use the already written logic for the Apple Watch, we need to examine the Weathery project. Let's have a look at the project navigator (Figure 2-1).

Figure 2-1. *"Weathery" project navigator*

By quickly going over the existing folders, we can see a few things:

- The iOS team organized some of the files by their **operational part**. We can see a dedicated folder for view controllers, another one for views, and so on.

- Regardless of the previous point, we can also see **different services** – we see folders for a network, analytics, and persistent store.

- Since we **don't see any business logic folders**, we assume the view controllers hold most of the app's logic.

This may look like a big mess, but we do see a pattern here. The Weathery team organized (Figure 2-2) their code.

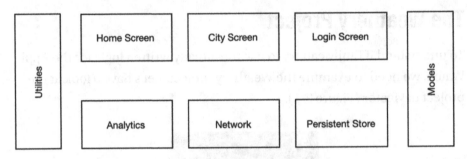

Figure 2-2. *Weathery project organization*

This may be an intuitive way to organize files, but not always the efficient one. Regarding the new mission to develop an Apple Watch version, managing your project can make it challenging to maintain it over time. Emily needs to rethink about reorganizing its project in a different way, a more efficient one.

Code Organization

We can't say the Weathery project code is not organized, but we indeed have a better way to manage our code and make it more **reusable and stable**. To reveal how to do that, we need to understand a few essential principles, some of them are probably familiar to you.

Note   Right now, I don't want to talk about any technical terms such as frameworks, libraries, and modules. We need to understand the theory first.

Separation of Concerns

Separation of concerns (SoC) is one of the most crucial principles when talking about software design. SoC means two things:

– Each component, a function, or a class has **only one responsibility**.

– Two components or two functions **cannot share** the same responsibility.

Separation of concerns is a key component when talking about a modular app. We already know we should write small functions that their goal is to do one task only. We also realize that's the case with classes. We don't always understand that this principle is also valid in a full module or a library.

One of the best ways to assimilate this is to move out of the computer science world and go to real life. It may sound weird, but yes, SoC is also valid in examples from the real world. In fact, it's vital for planning many projects and infrastructures.

Let's take a standard house and try to break it to different components with different responsibilities.

So, we've got a house – the house provides us a place to stay and live. We don't plan a house to be a public place, an office, or a shop – the house has only one mission. Inside the house, we have rooms – each room has its own responsibility. The bathroom is where we clean and wash – after all, we don't have a bed in our bathroom. The bedroom is the place for our private tasks – sleeping and changing clothes.

Every detail, every tool, and every furniture are there to support this fact.

But it doesn't stop in the "rooms" level. We can continue to "break" our house to more subcomponents – the sink in the bathroom is for washing our hands and face, not for dishes, and the closet in our bedroom is for clothes, not for our working tools.

11

What will happen if we try to give a component in our house more than one responsibility? What if we want to cook in our bathroom? Or sleep in the kitchen? Obviously, it isn't a good idea. Each room has its mission, a goal, and it is the best one in doing that specific task. We can describe the house structure as in Figure 2-3.

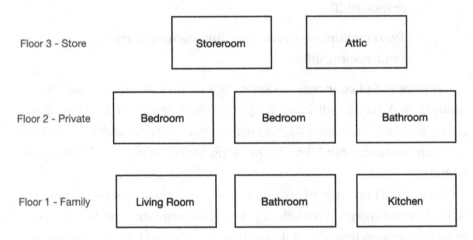

Figure 2-3. *A house diagram*

So, we can apply the same logic from our house structure to program design. Our program/app is built out of components that have their own responsibility, and they are themselves can be a part of a bigger component that also has a bigger task.

But where do we start? What floors come first? Or, maybe the question is – how many floors do we have in our app?

Presentation, Business, and Services

Now that we understand what separation of concerns is, let's try to look at our app from a bird's-eye view and understand the primary components our app is built on top of.

Some developers try to separate their app to features – login/ registration, main screen, settings screen, search, and so on.

While it seems reasonable, it doesn't really help us to **scale and maintain** our project in the long run. First, our app can have dozens of features, and we can **lose control** of our architecture. Second, surely some of the features will have to **share some core components**. Persistent store and network are easy to talk about, but what about business logic or other services? Coupling everything into a "feature" does not make it easier. And third, **what exactly is a "feature"?** Is it a screen? Or maybe it's an app capability like "sharing" or "in-app purchase"?

A "feature" is something hard to define precisely. Therefore, it might not be the right candidate for separation.

It All Starts with Data Flow

But maybe, there is a more logical way to look at our app, for example, through its data flow. Now, data flow doesn't mean music streaming or file download. Data flow is the **path for the information** to move from one part of the app to another.

Let's examine the "tapping on a button" action:

- The user taps a button.

- The view controller passes the event to the view model.

- The view model prepares the model and passes it to some class that decides what to do with the new information.

- From this point, the data can go to the core data or to our server using the URLSession.

Let's try to look at it in Figure 2-4, with more examples.

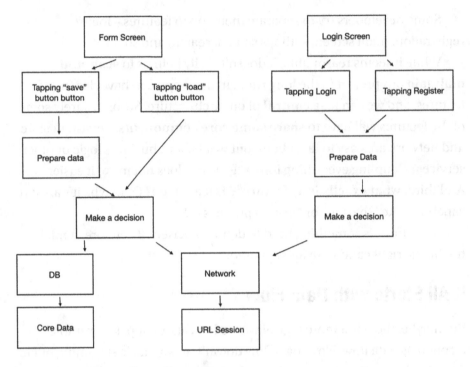

Figure 2-4. *Data flow diagram*

In Figure 2-4, we can see the different components and the arrows that show how the data moves around the app.

The Three-Layer Architecture

If you look at the diagram and try to find a repeated pattern, you can conclude that the data flow is going through three main components:

– It starts in the UI, where tapping on a button generates a data object we can work with. We call it the **presentation layer** or the **UI layer**. If you are aware of design patterns like MVVM/VIPER, the whole design pattern is considered part of the UI layer.

- Afterward, the data object goes to a component that needs to decide what to do with it. We call it the **business layer**. The business layer doesn't have to be a singleton – but it holds some logic that can be relevant for the type of UI, device, or platform.

- At the end of the flow, the data is sent to the server or the local persistent store (in this case, Core Data). It can also connect the data to a third-party library. We call it the **service layer** or the **data layer**.

Most of the client apps, not only on iOS but also on mobile, work this way – some action on the UI, a decision, and a service that handles the data. It is called the **three-layer architecture**, and it is popular among many systems and applications.

Note   Some call this architecture the "N-layer architecture" because, in some cases, you have more than three layers. You can also find it under the name of "three-tier" architecture, but when talking about iOS, this is a mistake – it is common to call "tier" to a layer that is physically separated. In our case, a "layer" is the better term to use.

Let's take a look at Figure 2-5 in an even more abstract way.

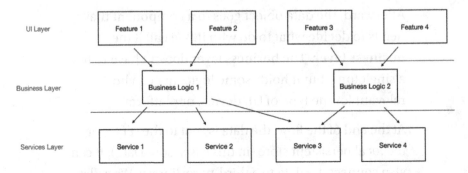

Figure 2-5. *Three-layer architecture*

Organizing our app to three layers has enormous benefits in terms of scalability and maintenance. Let's name some of them.

Note   The following list is crucial to understand the benefits of using Swift Packages in your projects. Swift Packages take these benefits and just leverage them.

Problems to Mini Problems

We all know that solving a small problem is more comfortable than solving a big one. So, breaking our app ("the problem") to layers makes it easier to handle the different steps of our data flow.

And this is not just a marketing statement.

You might think it's mainly relevant to your app's development stage, but in fact, in the development stage, breaking your app to different layers has a less significant effect.

Debugging, testing, and adding more capabilities are the parts where your app's separation really shines.

Because the data is moving between distinguishing layers, it's easier to catch bugs and issues, and because each layer has a different responsibility, it becomes simpler to write tests. **Smaller problems are easier to solve.**

But it doesn't have to end in the architecture level – the UI layer, while separated from the business logic and the service layer, can be severed to smaller problems (just like the house example I mentioned earlier). As a matter of fact, separating your app to smaller problems is a **recursive process** that can help you maintain your code over time. In the UI layer example, you can use all kinds of design patterns to build your UI layer, such as MVC, MVVM, VIPER, and so on. It is another separation, and in this case, it helps you handle the most sophisticated UI designs.

And of course, the design pattern you choose for your UI component can also be split into small files and so on.

Stability

Some inflatable boats are constructed with multiple air chambers. The reason is apparent – if one of the chambers loses its air pressure for some reason, the other chambers make sure the boat doesn't sink. The **modular** structure of inflatable boats makes them more **stable and safer** to use (take a look at Figure 2-6).

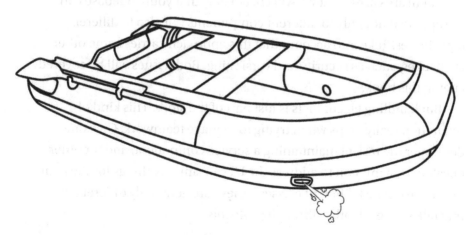

Figure 2-6. *An inflatable boat with a puncture*

Think of your code as an inflatable boat and your bugs as low air pressure (or worse, a puncture).

It's easier to replace and fix a damaged component in your codebase than trying to fix a broadside bug.

The image of modular apps to an inflatable boat can be applied to other objects from the real world as well, from machines, cars, houses, weapons, and more.

Modular objects narrow the damage to a particular component and can help fix the issue quickly and simply.

Teamwork

We all had to deal with git conflicts in our projects when trying to work as a team. Git conflicts result from two or more developers editing the same code line, and we all know that sometimes it is unavoidable.

But separating your app to different components reduces the number of potential conflicts.

Sure, it has a lot to do with the way your team works, but in the end, most chances your developers will work on different classes or even various modules/libraries and connect only with protocols.

There are cases (that we will cover later) that your codebase can be separated not only to different components but also to different repositories. Take into account that this approach carries some other challenges, such as security and versioning. Both issues will be covered later in this book.

But handling git conflicts is just part of the story. This kind of separation really helps when trying to manage teamwork. Give one developer the task of maintaining a service component, and for other developers, a mission to address the UI can simplify things for the team. These are not just different classes – these are genuinely different worlds that talk with each other through protocols.

Build Time

Build time is a painful topic.

To understand why build time is affected by the architecture you choose, we need to know how incremental build works.

When we make changes in a specific file, other files that depend on the particular files must recompile. The same goes for more files that depended on the recompiled files and so on.

Notice I didn't mention changes in classes, structs, or enums, but files. That's because it is entirely valid in Swift to add multiple entities in the same file. In this case, change in one entity requires the recompilation of the whole file.

Now, of course, this is true for any architecture you choose to build your app.

So, what is so special about three-layer architecture? This architecture makes sure the dependencies are configured in a way that fits your work and the scale of your project.

When you make changes in the network layer, you recompile the UI or even the logic that depended on it.

But it's not the same when working on a top layer like a UI layer.

When your dependencies are laid according to your data flow, it eases your compile process and can help you achieve better build times in the future.

Also, encapsulating some of the layers in a package of their own like we will learn shortly in this book can guide the compiler to optimize its build.

In short, compilers **love** code separation. Let's give it to them.

Redesign Our App Architecture

After the meeting with her boss, Emily felt helpless. She understood now that her iOS project is not ready for these kinds of changes.

Yes, the code was organized beautifully in folders, but that was it. Too much logical code was located in the UI, and besides the network layer, there wasn't any central place that could be shared with other clients. She read some great articles about app architecture, but this is an old project with over 1000 classes. Where does she start?

This is not uncommon – we have an existing, messy project, and we want to reorganize and separate it into UI, business, and services. How do we start?

We need to do a few steps, which are common both for reorganizing our project and building it from scratch.

First, we need to **draw our project architecture** on a paper or on a whiteboard.

We need to talk about our layers and decide what **design patterns** we are going to use.

And finally, we need to decide what **entities** we're going to have in each layer and the **protocols** our layers use to communicate.

Take a Paper and Draw a UML

A paper? When are we in the 1980s?

No. But sometimes it's useful to take good habits from the past. Paper and pen have one fantastic feature – they have barely any constraints when trying to spill your thoughts and draw them. With this method, the path from your brain to a visual thought presentation is concise.

And what you need to do right now is to draw a basic UML of your app essential components as you see them.

Some guides:

- We always start with the **apparent and straightforward** components. Afterward, it will be easier to complete the others. Usually, it means starting with one of the sides – services or UI.

- Before drawing, try to **make a list** on the side – all UI screens and all the "others" – network, DB, and more.

- Take into account **any third-party** libraries you might have.

- Try to **locate any global** variables, constants, structs, and functions, and understand what the missing components are.

Figure 2-7 shows a basic UML drawn on a paper.

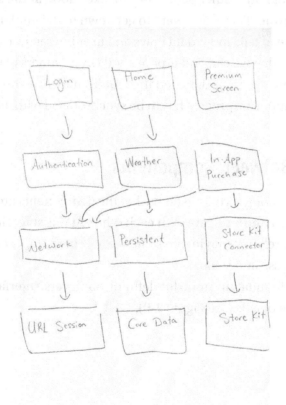

Figure 2-7. *A UML drawn on a paper*

Do This in Collaboration

In most cases, drawing a basic diagram on a paper or on a whiteboard can collaborate with our teammates. Studies show that different people have a different perspective on how systems are built, and they observe and analyze them differently.

Some people are more "attached" and feel natural **with the bottom layers**, meaning the services. They tend to be more involved in the implementation details and integration with other libraries.

On the other hand, other people like to take a **look at the system from the preceding one**. They don't want to get down to the implementation details but instead talk about data flows and user interaction.

This means that we can add product and QA members to the discussion to ensure we understand the requirements and how the data moves in our app. This process has to be synchronized with all the relevant people.

Relations Between Components

It is essential not only to understand what the components are but also **to connect and communicate** with each other. At this stage, it is enough to mention the relationship in one sentence – "fetch data," "save data," "receive progress," and so on.

This is the foundation stone for defining our layers' interfaces when we get down to the details (see Figure 2-8).

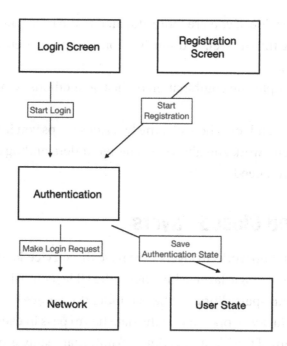

Figure 2-8. *Components' relations*

It is also a tool to figure out what is the primary goal of each component. If we see a component that does different tasks, we might consider splitting it, to keep the principle of "separation of concerns."

What Side to Start?

When we try to represent our three-layer system, we always have the question – on what side do we start?

Are we starting on placing all the UI screens and continuing down to the very bottom layers?

Or maybe the opposite – encapsulate all the services to components, build upon them the business logic, and connect the UI?

As I mentioned earlier, there is no clear answer to that. If you have a good understanding of your app's low-level implementation, it is perfectly normal to start your diagram with the service layer.

On the other side, if you are more attached to the user flows, you can start by drawing the UI layer, and starting from this point, derive the rest of the architecture.

For most people, the combination of the two methods is the winning path.

Moving back and forth between the two sides keeps you in context with the app framework and gives you a better understanding of what business logic you need.

Opened and Closed Layers

We said that our app works in layers – we have the **service layer**, which serves the business logic layer, which helps the UI layer finish its tasks. We also have third-party libraries that sit under the service layer. In general, our data flow works so that the data has to pass in each layer to get to the bottom of the hierarchy. But we know that reality is much more complicated than that. We definitely have situations that we have to **skip** a layer.

For example, we might have a business logic component that works directly with a third-party library or a UI presenter that works with the DB layer and skips the business logic component.

This is not ideal, but it sure can happen.

In these situations, it is essential to define if a layer can be "skipped" or do we have to pass it through.

A layer that can be skipped is called an "**opened**" layer.

If we have to pass it, it is called a "**closed**" layer.

Why does it matter?

If you remember from earlier, we discussed the principle of "separation of concerns."

As a reminder, the separation of concerns states that each component has one responsibility, which is responsible only by this component.

For example, if we have a layer that handles the calls to the DB and we want to bypass it and call the DB directly from a business logic layer, we, in fact, violate the principle of "separation of concerns."

There are times that we have to make compromises. For example, we want to prioritize simplicity over separations. In this case, it is important to define it and be aware of that.

Define Design Patterns

What is the difference between architecture and design patterns? This is a widespread confusion many developers (even seniors) have.

Remember my "house" example? So sorry, but I'm going to use it again.

Architecture is the skeleton of the house. It's the decision how many floors it has or if it has a basement or an attic.

The house's architecture can also define the primary purpose of each floor and how people can move from floor to floor – elevator or stairs.

So, what is the design pattern in this metaphor?

A design pattern is the internal structure of each floor – how many rooms, where are the doors, the furniture, or any general design decisions.

Going back to software design, architecture is how our app is built, its outline. The layers are the "house floors," and the interfaces between them are the stairs.

A design pattern is how each floor is built.

Think of a design pattern as a tool that can help you **solve common problems**. For example, to solve UI problems, you can pick one of MVC/ MVVM/MVP/VIPER design patterns.

For business logic, you can choose a façade or decorator.

A design pattern is also a solution for **communication between layers**, for example, choosing between closures, delegates, or notifications. See Figure 2-9.

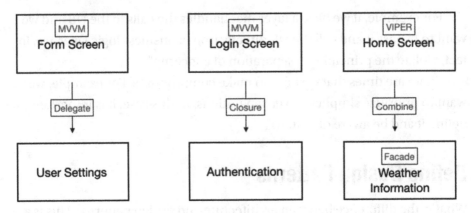

Figure 2-9. *Design patterns as part of the planning*

While design patterns are internal, it's important for our planning because it completes the final picture when discussing architecture. It brings everything in context in both ways and laying the ground for better decisions.

Define Your Entities

What are entities? Entities are the way we **keep information** in memory. Because we want to create a full separation between our components, we also want to define a **different entity** for each layer to leverage our components' flexibility.

For example, the data layer can generate a particular struct to hold the information fetched from the data store, and when the business logic reads it, it converts it to a different type, more comfortable to manipulate. The same goes for the UI layer, which probably needs to work with a different kind of information suitable for its needs. Take a look at Figure 2-10.

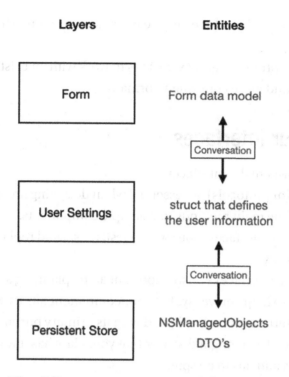

Figure 2-10. *The different components and their entities*

Using different entity in different layers has several advantages:

– First, this way, our components **truly decouple** from each other. You can even reuse a component in a different project and only need to convert the entity once.

– We know that each layer has a different goal and different concern. This means that each layer has different **needs**. Using the same entity structure is not only coupling the layers, but it also makes it hard for them to make use of the entity for their internal implementation. Converting the entity to a more convenient, purpose-specific form can help the layer achieve better performance and efficiency.

Notice you don't have to really "create" a new structure when a new data is receiving.

You can use protocols and extensions to work with an existing entity, but in a better and more convenient format.

Define Your Interfaces

Last but not least are the interfaces.

Interfaces (or protocols) are essential when designing architectures. They're one of the main methods to decouple components.

Working with interfaces is our way to test, reuse, and replace components easily.

Defining the interfaces is also important at the planning stage because it's a great tool to help you verify that your component fills its goal. The component interface has to be aligned with its primary purpose, and by thinking ahead, you might discover that your class has few more responsibilities and has to be split.

Defining interfaces can help you understand your component's real mission and also your data flow.

Summary

We learned why separating your app into layers is so important in many aspects. But it is also a precondition for starting to implement Swift Packages in your project and to build an excellent foundation for your codebase.

CHAPTER 3

Swift Package to Rescue

The most beautiful house in the world is the one you build yourself.

—Witold Rybczynski

In the previous chapter, we covered the basics of modular apps. Now it's time to get our hands dirty and dive into the technical details of creating and building Swift Packages.

In this chapter, you will learn

- What modules, libraries, and frameworks are

- What a Swift Package is and how it is built

- How to create a package from the command line and Xcode

- How to build and compile a package

First, let's go back to our Weathery team members who are scratching their heads and trying to understand what to do next.

© Avi Tsadok 2021
A. Tsadok, *Mastering Swift Package Manager*,
https://doi.org/10.1007/978-1-4842-7049-3_3

In the Meeting Room

The iOS team at Weathery is a small team of three teammates. They sat together and tried to plan their next moves.

"Ok, so we already have a network client as a set of classes. But even if we do the same for all the other services, how can we share them with the Apple Watch?", Kyle said. Kyle was the senior iOS developer of the team. He started to work at Weathery from the very beginning and knows every single line of code.

"Maybe we can assign them to the Apple Watch extension target. That should work," Kyle continued. "It's just a few mouse clicks."

"I don't know, that doesn't feel right," Emily responded. "What happens if we want to add more files? We need to mark them too. It sounds like an awkward idea. There must be a better, more elegant way."

"I heard there's something called Package that lets you easily do that. But I don't know how to use it; I need to learn," said Joshua, the team junior developer. "Give me an hour to play with it, and I'll return with some information."

Let's Start with Terminology

Modules, frameworks, SDKs, packages, and libraries – these are all terms that we, as developers, are likely to bump into in our day-to-day lives. If we want to become a master in Swift Packages, we first need to understand what they mean.

A disclaimer   There are differences with the meaning of those terms among different languages and platforms. We'll focus on Apple platforms' meaning.

Module

iOS and Mac projects are built upon different parts that we call modules. When you start a new, fresh project, your app is built upon one module – the app itself.

In the previous chapter, we discussed how much it's essential to build a modular app, and now we can point out what modules are.

Well, libraries, frameworks, and Swift Packages are all types of modules, and these are all tools that help us separate our code and make it more reusable.

Library

One type of module that we have is a *library*. A library contains a set of classes that have a shared goal. For example, a library can handle a specific logic for a game. It can also handle database integration or network requests.

In iOS, there are two types of libraries – **dynamic** and **static**.

The type of library defines how it links to the app.

Static libraries are linked to your app during compilation time. They become part of your app and increase your build size. If you see a file with an ".a" extension, that will be a static library.

Unlike static libraries, *dynamic* libraries are linked to your app during runtime. They are **not** part of your build but have a negative influence on your startup time. Because dynamic libraries link to your app during runtime, you can replace them without shipping a new build. This is why dynamic libraries are not supported in iOS, besides Apple's own system libraries.

Dynamic libraries also have their file extension – it is ".dylib," and you probably met these types of files when linking system libraries.

Framework

A *framework* might sound like an advanced, complicated technology to some developers, but it is really just a folder that encapsulates resources, code, and other libraries, both dynamic and static.

In Apple platforms, you can find frameworks as folders with the extension of ".framework."

You might be wondering, "what is the difference between a library and a framework?" Well, there are some technical differences. For example, libraries produce something called an object file, a binary representation of its code. When frameworks are mostly just folders with code and data, some of them are libraries themselves.

We'll talk about more important differences later in this book.

Swift Package

Swift Package is somehow similar to a library, although it is not compiled. This kind of library is also a set of classes aimed to solve a particular logic problem, but Swift Package makes packaging and testing processes much more comfortable and straightforward.

However, there are some unique identifiers to Swift Packages. Let's go over them.

Code Location

Like CocoaPods, the source code of the package is designed to be **located in another location**. This means you can place your code in another location in your local repository or even on a remote git repository.

This can help you share your code between projects and help your team work in parallel on different parts of your code.

Dependencies

Another thing is the dependencies. When you work with static libraries, you need to **manage their dependencies** by yourself. And this means not only their dependencies but also their dependencies' dependencies. It is a recursive process, which sits solely on the developer responsibility. But a Swift Package is part of Swift Package Manager (SPM) that handles all of that for you, just like CocoaPods and Carthage.

Platform and System Version

Swift Package Management doesn't end only with dependencies – a package can have more requirements, for example, **a relevant platform and a minimum system version**. This can help the compiler notify you when the package you are trying to use is not suitable for your project.

And just like dependencies, Swift Package Manager verifies those requirements for you with all the dependencies' tree, something you need to do yourself with static and dynamic libraries.

Versioning

One of the most complicated tasks when dealing with libraries is to manage their versions. When your library is based on an external codebase that evolves over time, things can break and cause bugs. And when you have a dependency tree, the problem just gets bigger.

Fortunately, every Swift Package can lock its dependencies to a specific version. Not only that, you can even lock them to a particular branch or commit.

Versioning is a great tool that can help your app and your packages stay stable even if their dependencies get new, untested code.

Create Our First Package

Okay, enough with the talking. Now that we know what modules, libraries, frameworks, and packages are, it's time to create our first package.

Create a Package from the Command Line

We'll start with the basic tool we all have in our Macs – the Terminal.

Open your Terminal, create a new folder, and enter the following lines:

```
mkdir MyFirstSwiftPackage
cd MyFirstSwiftPackage
```

MyFirstSwiftPackage will be the name of your Swift Package folder – it doesn't have to be the name of the module that will be imported at the end and even not the name of the package itself, so feel free to choose any reasonable name of the folder.

The next step is to generate the package files, and for that, we have a simple line:

```
swift package init
```

The result is this:

```
Creating library package: MyFirstSwiftPackage
Creating Package.swift
Creating README.md
Creating .gitignore
Creating Sources/
Creating Sources/MyFirstSwiftPackage/MyFirstSwiftPackage.swift
Creating Tests/
Creating Tests/LinuxMain.swift
Creating Tests/MyFirstSwiftPackageTests/
```

```
Creating Tests/MyFirstSwiftPackageTests/
MyFirstSwiftPackageTests.swift
Creating Tests/MyFirstSwiftPackageTests/XCTestManifests.swift
```

Wow, how many files! To simplify it, let's look at our folder in a tree view:

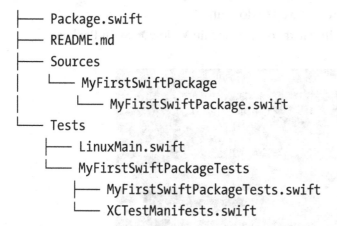

```
├── Package.swift
├── README.md
├── Sources
│      └── MyFirstSwiftPackage
│              └── MyFirstSwiftPackage.swift
└── Tests
        ├── LinuxMain.swift
        └── MyFirstSwiftPackageTests
                  ├── MyFirstSwiftPackageTests.swift
                  └── XCTestManifests.swift
```

Now, that's better. Let's see what do we have here:

Package.swift – That's the package manifest file. It describes the structure of the package, its requirements, targets, products, and dependencies.

Readme.md – This is a standard readme file. Here we can put our installation and usage documentation. It is also important when uploading to a git repository to display useful information to other developers.

Sources – This is the folder that contains the code of your package. If you notice, this folder includes another subfolder named MyFirstSwiftPackage. There is a subfolder for every target or executable (don't worry, we'll talk about all of it). To start, we have only one target.

Tests – If you read my book *Pro iOS Testing*, you should already know how much tests are essential to your code quality and stability. Luckily, every Swift Package comes with a tests folder and a dedicated target.

Xcode 11 and Swift Packages

Xcode 11, announced in 2019, brought a built-in integration with Swift
Package Manager. One of the features Xcode 11 (and above) has, is to
create (and manage) Swift Packages straight from Xcode. This is another
option to create a Swift Package instead of using the command line and
probably the more common way to do that.

To create a new Swift Package, choose File ➤New ➤ Swift Package….

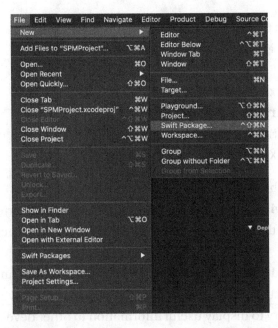

Figure 3-1. *Adding a new Swift Package from Xcode*

In the next dialog, just choose the project and group you want to add
the package to. You don't have to add the package to an existing project,
and you can add it as a project of its own.

After adding the package, we can see it in our project navigator with
the same structure we saw when doing the same action from the command
line.

Figure 3-2. *Swift Package in Xcode navigator*

As discussed, the way we configure the package is through its manifest file – the `Package.swift` file.

Package.swift

`Package.swift` is the manifest file for your project, and it contains the package's metadata. This is the place where you configure your package requirements and structure.

Let's open the `Package.swift` file that the `swift package init` command generated for us:

```
// swift-tools-version:5.3
// The swift-tools-version declares the minimum version of
Swift required to build this package.

import PackageDescription
```

```
let package = Package(
    name: "MyFirstSwiftPackage",
    products: [
        // Products define the executables and libraries a
        package produces, and make them visible to other
        packages.
        .library(
            name: "MyFirstSwiftPackage",
            targets: ["MyFirstSwiftPackage"]),
    ],
    dependencies: [
        // Dependencies declare other packages that this
        package depends on.
        // .package(url: /* package url */, from: "1.0.0"),
    ],
    targets: [
        // Targets are the basic building blocks of a package.
        A target can define a module or a test suite.
        // Targets can depend on other targets in this package,
        and on products in packages this package depends on.
        .target(
            name: "MyFirstSwiftPackage",
            dependencies: []),
        .testTarget(
            name: "MyFirstSwiftPackageTests",
            dependencies: ["MyFirstSwiftPackage"]),
    ]
)
```

Let's understand exactly how this file is built.

Swift Tools and PackageDescription

Don't be mistaken by the double slash you see in the following line:

```
// swift-tools-version:5.3
```

Although it looks like a comment, it is the row that determines the **Swift Tools version** your package manifest file is using.

Swift Tools comes with every version of Xcode and is parallel to the latest Swift version you have.

Even though every version might bring new features to Swift Package you can use, it doesn't mean you need to update all the other packages you already have to the latest version.

The good thing about Swift Tools is that you can keep the old code working with an old API and update it only when needed, just like in Figure 3-3.

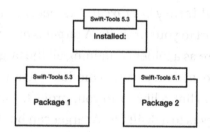

Figure 3-3. *Working with several versions of Swift Tools API*

The one thing you should notice is that it doesn't work oppositely. The Swift Tools version is the **minimum version** required to use the package, so you cannot integrate it with old versions of Xcode with an outdated Swift Tools version.

The next line imports the PackageDescription module:

```
import PackageDescription
```

The main class in the `PackageDescription` module is `Package`. The manifest file is responsible for initializing the Package object, which holds the package configuration information.

Now, if you look closely at your new Package file, you could see that it's not a new format or a language – it's just a familiar Swift code. All the configuration information is passed within the Package object initialization, so nothing here should be new to you.

Before we move to how to define the Package's file properties, we need to understand what products and targets are.

Products and Targets

When you imagine how you are going to use the created packages in your projects, you probably see something like

```
import MyLibrary
```

So, in this case, `MyLibrary` is a **target**. A target is an actual module you are going to import to your projects. A target is also represented in the package's file structure as a folder containing all the target files.

On the other hand, a library is not a module – it is a **group of modules** (or "targets"). After you link a library to your project, you get the ability to import all of its targets to a Swift file. A target can be shown in multiple libraries so that you can think of this relationship as "many-to-many" connections.

I know this part is a little bit confusing – there's a package that contains libraries, and these libraries have targets that at the end are the modules we use in our apps.

So, let's see how a package might look like (Figure 3-4).

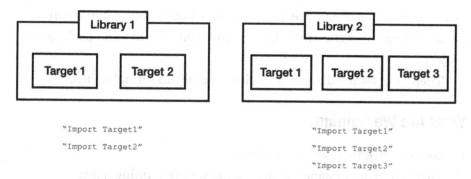

Figure 3-4. *A package "Libraries and Targets" structure*

Figure 3-4 is not everyday use in Swift Packages. In most cases, for each target, we'll have a matched library, and probably most packages you'll bump into will have one target (besides the testing target) and one library.

You can think of the combination of targets and libraries as another way you can modularize your code within the package itself.

Targets are the "lower level" of your package architecture, and the libraries are the "top level."

One good example can be a package that handles "helper" functions. You can create many targets – one that handles dates, one for colors, texts, numbers, and more.

And for the libraries, you can group those targets to libraries in a more sense way.

For example, you can create a library called "Primitives" and group texts and numbers targets.

Library is what you **link** to your project, and its targets are what you **import** to your files.

Naming

The first property is the name.

You might be wondering why I'm making a big deal out of the naming part. In my opinion, naming plays a significant role in creating an expressive and clean code. But it is even a bigger issue when talking about Packages designed to be implemented and use in other packages or projects.

Therefore, we need to pay attention carefully to several points.

What Are We Naming?

It's not that obvious as you might think.

We need to understand precisely **what we are naming**. I just mentioned that in addition to a `Package`, there are also `Libraries` and `Targets`.

I didn't mention that we also have the git repository we might want to upload the package to and the main classes that the package might contain. So, in the case of `Package.swift`, we are naming the Package only. We can give other names to the libraries, the targets, and the git repo we may want to use, but this is done in other places.

Be Consistent

There are several naming conventions we can use:

- UpperCamelCase

- lowerCamelCase

- snake_case

- dash-case

And these are relevant to more areas in programming other than Swift Packages.

It is important to be consistent with your choice. Consistency helps your "users" (and by "users" I mean other developers, of course) to dive into your code or your package much faster.

Having said that, there are unwritten rules or recommendations in that area.

It is acceptable that packages and target names have **UpperCamelCase** name conventions, and the git repository name can be a **dash-case**, for example, if you have a package named MyLibrary:

Package name: MyLibrary

Git repository name: https://github.com/avitsadok/my-library

A consistent naming paradigm helps other developers, and even you, read code faster and expect a specific format when integrating other classes and modules.

Be Meaningful

Let's face it – MyLibrary is a lousy example of a package name. It doesn't describe anything about the package functionality except it is "My" library... so, your package needs to have a specific, clear name that describes the package functionality and its goal.

StringTools, as a name, is not specific enough. StringSearchingTools, on the other hand, is much more distinct.

Giving the right name to a package can also reduce issues described in the next point.

Be Unique

This is a pain point. Every Swift Package has an identity, and we cannot use **two packages with the same identity** in the same project. And what is the package's identity? You guessed right – its name.

You can conclude from this that picking a unique name for your package is not only important, it is also essential in some cases.

There are many discussions in the Swift community on how to solve this issue. Some suggest that name identity can be the git repository URL, but this solution also has open questions.

Another solution might be adding some sort of an ID or an origin property, and perhaps it will happen in one of the future Swift versions.

For now, a pragmatic solution can be adding a prefix to the package name, with the developer's initials.

For example, instead of `StringSearchingTools`, we can call it `ATStringsSearchingTools`.

Even though it doesn't look like an elegant name convention, it may solve your big headaches in the future.

Platforms

Swift supports five platforms – iOS, macOS, tvOS, watchOS, and Linux at the time of this writing.

Just like any other code in your app, Packages also have minimum OS version requirements.

The `platforms` property contains the list of the minimum supported versions for the different platforms.

The property itself is an array of structs; each describes a platform and a minimum version.

Let's see an example of such a property:

```
platforms: [.iOS(.v11), .macOS(.v10_15), .watchOS(.v5)],
```

I think it is easy to see that this package has a minimum iOS version requirement 11 and above, macOS version 10.15 and above, and watchOS version 5 and above.

What happens if we don't mention a platform on the list? Can we still use this package on this specific platform?

Apparently, yes.

The platform's property doesn't describe the **supported** platforms. All platforms are supported. If we don't add a minimum version for a specific platform, the actual minimum version will be the first that supports Swift.

For instance, if we don't add the iOS version to the list, the minimum version will be iOS 8.

It is better to try and set minimum versions as lower as we can. And if we can avoid setting a minimum, it's even better. Remember, the minimum version is a constraint that can make it difficult for us to integrate our package with other packages or projects.

Creating a SupportedPlatform struct is easy – the struct has a list of static functions that can help you generate a minimum version.

We have two options to create a supported platform struct – you can pass a constant that describes the specific version you want to support or give a String version.

In this function, you need to pass a constant:

```
public static func iOS(_ version: PackageDescription.
SupportedPlatform.IOSVersion) -> PackageDescription.
SupportedPlatform

// and the use is something like that:
SupportedPlatform.iOS(.v11)
```

And this is the function that requires a version as String:

```
public static func iOS(_ versionString: String) ->
PackageDescription.SupportedPlatform

// this is the usage example:
SupportedPlatform.iOS("11.0.0")
```

By looking at the generated interface of the PackageDescription file, you can see the list of the constants you can use:

```
public struct IOSVersion : Encodable {

    public static let v8: PackageDescription.
    SupportedPlatform.IOSVersion

    public static let v9: PackageDescription.
    SupportedPlatform.IOSVersion
```

```
    public static let v10: PackageDescription.
    SupportedPlatform.IOSVersion

    public static let v11: PackageDescription.
    SupportedPlatform.IOSVersion

    public static let v12: PackageDescription.
    SupportedPlatform.IOSVersion
}
```

Dependencies

We have a whole chapter discussing dependencies, and every developer that had to deal with any sort of dependency manager knows that it's a central topic.

Your project can use your packages' code, but your package cannot use other project code, except for other packages.

Those "other packages" can be located either locally or in another remote git repository when Swift Package Manager is responsible for cloning and linking it to your project.

As mentioned earlier, cloning, updating, and linking other packages defined as dependencies **is a recursive process**. It aims to save you as a developer hard work of taking care of versions, compatibility issues, and more.

Defining a remote dependency is easy. We just add a new entry to the dependencies array:

```
dependencies: [
    .package(url: "https://github.com/avitsadok/example-
    package-common.git", .exact("2.0.0")
]
```

The first thing you notice here is how easy and straightforward it is to add a new dependency.

Before building the project, the Swift Package Manager tries to resolve all the packages' dependencies. In this process, it makes sure all the dependencies are downloaded and linked to your app.

In the preceding code snippet, we can see that **we can also set a constraint** for that dependency – we require the dependency to be exactly version 2.0.0.

We do that to prevent unexpected changes to the package we are linking that may affect our code.

In the next chapters, we'll learn how to add other constraints to the dependency configuration, such as a branch or a specific commit.

Working on Our Package

"Hey Emily, I read about creating a Swift Package. It looks awesome!" Joshua said to Emily. "I played with it a little bit, and generating a new package is very easy, both from the command line and Xcode. What do we do next?"

"Let me think," Emily responded.

Emily's primary concern is creating a local package as part of the project or creating a new git repository with a new project and work separately.

"I want the Swift Package to be isolated from the rest of the project. I'm wondering if that can be achieved within our project. Can you do some research on what is best for us? A new project or adding the package as part of our project?"

The concern Emily has is based on her instincts. She senses that creating a separated module has additional meanings – building, compiling, linking, and testing.

One thing to notice about Swift Packages is that they are easy to use. It is effortless to create one (we already know how to do that), but it's even easier to work on them.

We don't have to maintain and develop our Package on another project or repository. We can do that **as part of our existing project**.

In fact, we can compile and build our package, regardless of our project, and the main executable is even compiled!

Building

One easy way to build a package is from the command line:

```
→  $swift build
[4/4] Merging module Common
```

`swift build` command looks short and straightforward, but underneath, it is quite sophisticated and powerful.

Where `swift build` runs, it downloads all the dependencies defined in the `Package.swift` file, verifies their requirements, and compiles them. This process happens recursively to all the dependencies' tree.

If one of the requirements fails along the way, the process is terminated.

We can also test our package straight from the command line using the `swift test` command:

```
→  SP swift test
Test Suite 'All tests' started at 2020-10-23 16:54:53.145
Test Suite 'SP3PackageTests.xctest' started at 2020-10-23
16:54:53.146
Test Suite 'SPTests' started at 2020-10-23 16:54:53.146
Test Case '-[SPTests.SPTests testExample]' started.
Test Case '-[SPTests.SPTests testExample]' passed (0.051 seconds).
Test Suite 'SPTests' passed at 2020-10-23 16:54:53.198.
        Executed 1 test, with 0 failures (0 unexpected) in
        0.051 (0.051) seconds
```

```
Test Suite 'SP3PackageTests.xctest' passed at 2020-10-23
16:54:53.198.
      Executed 1 test, with 0 failures (0 unexpected) in 0.051
      (0.051) seconds
Test Suite 'All tests' passed at 2020-10-23 16:54:53.198.
      Executed 1 test, with 0 failures (0 unexpected) in 0.051
      (0.052) seconds
```

We'll go over testing later in this book, but you can already see how simple it is to test your package with just one short line.

Building from Xcode

Building our package from the Terminal is easy, but we, as iOS developers, spend most of our time using Xcode, not the command line.

The good news is that we can build and test Swift Packages directly from Xcode, starting with Xcode 11.

Creating a New Package from Xcode

To create a new Swift Package in Xcode, choose File ➤ New ➤ Swift Package.

A new dialog appears, asking you to choose a location for our package (Figure 3-5).

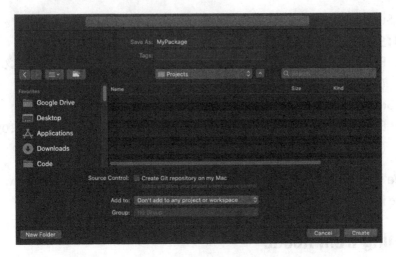

Figure 3-5. *Adding a new Swift Package from Xcode*

If you notice, at the bottom of the dialog, there are two more options – adding to a project and its group.

Like many technical settings, this one represents the workflow you want to work with.

If you choose to add this Swift Package to an existing project, the Swift Package will be an integrated part of the project. This one is suitable for taking **some logic in an existing project** and encapsulating it in a package. In most cases, that will be the preferred method.

The package will be part of the project file tree, and working on it is part of working on the project.

The second option is to add a stand-alone package, not related to a specific project or workspace. This package can be uploaded to git later if desired.

A stand-alone package is more fitting when creating some logic **planned to be used in various projects** or released as an open source project.

In that case, the working on the package will be in a separate window and not part of any project or workspace.

In both cases, you will see the package in your project navigator window, marked in a special "Package" icon (see Figure 3-6).

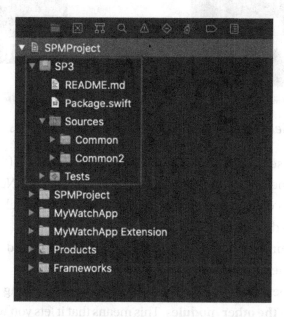

Figure 3-6. *The Swift Package in the project navigator*

Once Xcode recognizes that one of its folders is a Swift Package, it marks it with a special icon. The recognition is done using the Package. swift file.

As part of the continuous process of project indexing, Xcode is trying to resolve the package dependencies and configuration each time you open the project or make changes to the Package.swift manifest file or one of the package classes.

For each library Xcode identified in the package, it generates a scheme to help you build the library directly from Xcode Scheme Menu (see Figure 3-7).

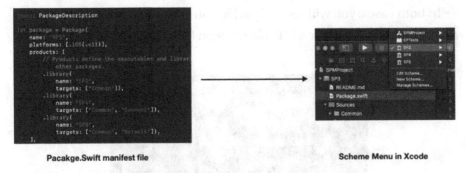

Pacakge.Swift manifest file   **Scheme Menu in Xcode**

Figure 3-7. *Generated schemes for the different libraries*

As you can see, there is no scheme for the package itself ("SP3"). Also, there are no schemes for the different targets ("Common," "Network"); that's because it doesn't make sense to work on an individual target when the product we deliver is the library itself.

Once the library scheme is selected, it is possible to build and test it just like any other module.

One of the benefits of working with packages is that building its library is **separated from the other modules**. This means that it lets you work on part of your codebase without the rest of your project that can even be compiled.

Compiling the library alone may sound like a small issue, but it is actually a significant change in our workflow.

Instead of looking at our project as one giant codebase, we need to see it as small logical services that can be developed separately and integrated later on.

It has a big influence on how the team works and maintains its apps.

Summary

In this chapter, we've learned the different terms. We also learned how a package is built and how to create one and build it, both from the Terminal and Xcode.

The next thing our team needs to learn is how to integrate their new package to the app, covered in the next chapter.

CHAPTER 4

Design and Link Our First Package

Consider thinking of architectural decisions as investments and take into account the associated rate of return, it is a useful approach for finding out how pragmatic or fit for purpose every option on the table is.

—Richard Monson-Haefel

In the previous chapter, we learned the basic terms and how to create our first Swift Package, both from the command line and Xcode.

We need to know how to integrate it with our project and design a good API that can serve not only other developers but also ourselves.

In this chapter, you will learn

- How to link your Swift Package with your project

- How to plan your library interface

- How to decide about the different access levels

- What is a scenario-driven design

© Avi Tsadok 2021
A. Tsadok, *Mastering Swift Package Manager*,
https://doi.org/10.1007/978-1-4842-7049-3_4

- How to name your methods and classes to be clear and consistent

- How to document your code using markup language in comments

What Do We Do Next?

"I made it!", Joshua came to Emily, excited. "I created our first Swift Package. It is a network library, and it contains all of our network queries and requests. Creating the library was very easy. For now, we have one library and one target. I think that should be enough."

"Great!", said Emily. "Did you try to integrate it with the app?"

Joshua seemed to be a little bit uncomfortable.

"Well, I tried. For some reason, it's not working as expected."

"What do you mean?" Emily asked.

"I created the package as part of the project, just like we said. But when I try to import the module to one of our classes and use it, it says 'No such module."

"Did you ask Kyle's help?" Emily asked.

"Yes, he said that we use CocoaPods for integrating other modules. This is new to him as well."

Emily thought – if that's the case with our first Package, what will happen with the rest...?

Linking the Package Libraries

Emily has no justification for her concerns. Importing modules from a local Swift Package to an app is straightforward and requires only one prestep.

Note   This is the time to remind you again of the difference between a package and a library. A library packs one or more modules (or targets). A package contains one or more libraries.

After adding a package to your project, the next step is to link one (or more) of its libraries to your executable targets.

Since your project might contain different targets, such as Watch extensions, widgets, and Siri intents, it is obvious that not all of them have to be linked to your package code.

Linking a library is easy – under the target general settings tag, there is a section called "**Frameworks, Libraries, and Embedded Content**" (see Figure 4-1).

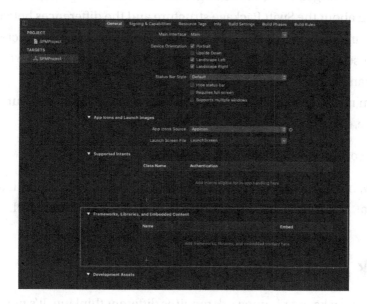

Figure 4-1. *Frameworks and Libraries section*

Pressing on the + button brings a dialog (Figure 4-2) that lists all Swift Packages currently found in your workspace or project.

Figure 4-2. Adding libraries from existing Swift Package

We need to pay attention for a moment to what we see in this window. Under the package name, you could see the **list of libraries**. When you link a library to a target, you give the target access to all library targets. When we talked about the Swift Package structure and the differences between libraries and targets, this is one of the places where it is being reflected.

After selecting one of the package libraries, we can see it in the list of linked frameworks and libraries.

From now on, we can import one of the package targets into our codebase, like this:

```
import common // "common" is a target
```

Now, how do we use the package? What is the right way to do that? To learn that, we need to understand how to design a good library API.

Think As a Service Provider

Creating a package or framework requires different thinking. It's not a coincidence that libraries are named "products" in Swift Packages – we are de facto creating products for various projects and apps.

As a result, we need to pay attention to our application programming interface (API) in all of its aspects.

Design a Good API

One of the biggest problems when developers code is that they live in a mindset that they write code for **personal use**.

Not only that, since it's fresh, things like function naming, comments, and error handling are left in the dark.

This problem is not related solely to Swift Packages or even API design – it also happens in standard classes. We write thousands of code lines – assuming that we can remember exactly what we meant when we wrote them in a naïve approach, even if it was just a week ago.

So, when you create your module, the first rule is to treat it like developing a product to be **used by hundreds of other developers**.

This approach can help you look at your code from a different perspective and help build a better, easily maintainable Swift Package.

Let's go over some of the ways and tips that can help you write a great package.

Think About the Developer As a Naïve One

Think about the developer, facing with your code, as a naïve developer. And if you think that this is unnecessary, think again. A few months later or even weeks, when you will try to use your code, you're becoming a naïve user yourself.

Take into account the most common use case of your package and make it super clear and straightforward.

Try to figure out what are the rare cases and make them possible.

But what exactly is a "naïve approach" or a "common use case"?

Let's take a look at the following code:

```
let networkClient = NetworkClient()
networkClient.prepare()
networkClient.requestURL(url : URL, completion:{dict in

        })
```

The preceding code describes a network client that makes a URL request. If you look closely, you can see a `prepare()` call just before the request. In this example, this is a required step to make sure the code performs correctly.

A "prepare" function is a common approach for a class's "lazy" setup. You can see it in many SDKs and even in Apple's own SDK.

But of course, there is an apparent downside here – the developer **needs to know** that he needs to add this step. Otherwise, the URL request won't work.

If the "prepare" function is not avoidable, we should treat the user as a naïve one that forgot to implement it.

One option can be **documentation** – remember, every package has its own `Readme` file. Fill in the readme file even if the package is for your use.

The second way to solve it is to use an **assertion** with a clear, informative message.

No matter what you choose, assume that the developer (even you!) forgot or didn't know about this step, and he is banging his head trying to figure out why your code just didn't work as expected.

Another thing that can help the developer understand how he needs to use your library can be through access control.

Access Control

Everything I mention here is vital to classes as well, but this one gets even more critical when talking about packages.

"Access control" defines what functions, classes, and enums we expose to the developer – this is what we refer to when we talk about private/open/public.

Many developers think that access control is essential because of performance optimization. Access control indeed has some influence on your runtime performance, but it's not the main reason we need to address it when building a library.

Access control helps us explain how to use our code. It marks the classes and functions the user can or should use and indicates the proper way to implement your library.

Marking classes and functions as private also makes sure the developer won't unintentionally use code that can damage or make his data corrupted.

Let's quickly go over the five levels of access control Swift has.

Private

The first one is private.

Private is the lowest and most restrictive level of control in Swift, and it prevents access from outside the scope of the method/variable, for example:

```
class A {

    private func testPrivate() {

    }
}

A().testPrivate() // doesn't have access
```

In the preceding example, the testPrivate() method is marked as private. Therefore, we cannot access it outside the class.

Even though private is not the default access level, we should **always mark methods and variables as private** unless we want to expose them outside the class.

fileprivate

Private is a great way to restrict access to your code, but sometimes we need a little more flexibility, for example, if we have a class that makes use of a dedicated struct.

In this struct, we want to mark some methods or variables as private but still want to give the class access to those methods without exposing them to other classes.

Because in situations like this, the class and the struct are often written in one file, we can allow access only to classes and structs **in the same file**, and it is called fileprivate.

fileprivate eases your work by allowing all objects to be accessed within the same file.

```
class A {

    fileprivate func testFilePrivate() {

    }
}

A().testFilePrivate() // we have access!
```

It's the same code as the private example, but now with a fileprivate access level.

This access level can "save" you from opening access to a class or a struct just because you need to access it from another place.

Open/Public

When talking about accessing classes and structs within the same module, fileprivate/private is solely relevant.

But when dealing with libraries and frameworks, additional access levels are joining the party.

The next access level above fileprivate is **internal**. "Internal" means that one cannot access the specific method/struct from outside the module. You don't have to mark a class or a method as internal – this is done by default.

```
class A {

    internal func testPrivate() {

    }

    func testPrivate() {

    }
}

A().testPrivate()
```

In the preceding code, you can see that I marked the method as internal, just like I did with private and fileprivate. But, as I said, all entities are internal by default, so it's up to you to choose if you want to mark them or not.

To expose entities from outside the module, we are going to use the **public** modifier.

The public modifier allows other modules to access a specific entity, and that's also the way we **define an API** for our module.

As mentioned earlier, marking entities and functions as a public helps us document our package.

Parameters, Return Type, and Properties in Public Access Level

One thing to notice in the Public access level is when we define a signature for a function, all of its parameters and return type **must be public as well**.

For example, take a look at the following code:

```
struct MessageItem {

}

public class MyPublicClass {

    public func showMessage(message : MessageItem) {
        print(str)
    }
}
```

In the preceding code snippet, MyPublicClass is declared as public, and its method showMessage is declared public as well. However, its message parameter is from the type MessageItem, which is currently declared internal.

This code cannot be compiled and requires us to update the access level of MessageItem to public. Of course, this is also true for class and struct properties – if you declare a property as public, you need to make sure its type definition is also public.

Public Constructor

Another thing we need to be aware of is the class or the struct constructor.

Look at the following code:

```
public class MyPublicClass {

    public func showMessage(message : MessageItem) {
        print(str)
    }
}
```

To use `MyPublicClass`, we need to create an instance, writing something like this:

```
let object = MyPublicClass()
```

We know that every Swift class has an `init()` function. But the `init` function is declared as `internal` by default.

This means you need to write your own `init` function and declare it as `public` to initialize your own object.

```
public init() { }
```

Now, it is perfectly legit to initialize `MyPublicClass` as it was done in the code earlier.

Access Level in Testing

We're going to discuss testing later in this book, but just to keep you calm at this stage, if you want to write unit tests for your library functions, you don't need to declare them as `public`, even though you access them from outside the module.

If you recall, when creating a test case, we import the module we want to test, and we prefix it with the `@testable` attribute.

What the `@testable` attribute does is **to leverage the access level** in the imported module.

In short, it means that the `internal` access level now becomes `public` and can be accessed for testing purposes only.

Of course, it still means you cannot test private methods directly. Private methods in testing are a different issue and are covered in my book *Pro iOS Testing* by Apress.

Scenario-Driven Design

So, where do we start? How do we implement the different approaches described earlier?

Many developers make the same mistake – they build their library **from bottom to top**.

It means they start with basic, small, logical functions and going up until they reach the public functions.

We already said that a library is a product. It means that we need to turn our perspective and start from our end user (in this case, the developer who will use our library). We need to imagine the most common use cases and development flows and start with writing the most suitable public functions.

Defining the different flows and use cases is also a tool that can help us not only focus our work on real-life scenarios but also narrow down our unit tests.

Let's try to imagine a library that deals with removing and adding HTML entities to a `String` variable.

At this stage, we don't care about **how** to implement such logic. We first need to imagine how the developer is going to utilize our library.

At first glance, we have three primary ways to accomplish that – a String extension, a logic function that returns a value, or a logic function with an `inout` parameter (remember, this is just an example).

In fact, we have additional ways to do that, but for now, I want to focus on these three options.

Three Different Ways Produce Three Different Experiences

Experience? It's just coding, isn't it? As a developer, you are probably aware of the fact that coding can be delightful and enjoyable, but it can also be cumbersome and annoying.

So yes, as a library creator, the experience your user (again, the developer) will have is up to you.

By using the three suggested ways described previously, we can provide different experiences to our end users.

Let's see that in action.

String extension:

```
let originalString = "Hello. <br> This is a string with
<b>HTML</b> entities"
let newString = originalString.stringByRemovingHTMLEntities()
```

A logic function with a return value:

```
let originalString = "Hello. <br> This is a string with
<b>HTML</b> entities"
let newString = StringUtils().getStringByRemovingHTMLEntities(o
riginalString: originalString)
```

A logic function with an inout parameter:

```
var originalString = "Hello. <br> This is a string with
<b>HTML</b> entities"
StringUtils().removeHTMLEntities(string: &originalString)
```

What are the main differences between these three approaches if they all provide the same functionality in the end?

At first glance, the differences may look minor, and maybe they are in the short run. But let's examine them a little bit deeper.

I'll start with the **extension method**. Extensions provide us a great, clean way to extend a given class's functionality, struct, or enum, without using subclassing or creating a new class/struct for that.

This results in an exquisite way of code writing.

On the other hand, there are some downsides of heavily using extensions in Swift, especially when implementing them in a Swift library.

If you choose to go with extensions in your library, you should think about what an end developer expects when he sees his code after a long period.

Look again at this Swift extension usage:

```
let newString = originalString.stringByRemovingHTMLEntities()
```

When looking at the code, `stringByRemovingHTMLEntities` looks like a natural part of the original `String` value type. If the developer is not familiar with implementing this code snippet, he can't tell whether it is part of the Swift language unless he right-clicks it in Xcode and reveals the source code.

And that leads us to the "dark side" of Swift extensions – the ability to understand where the logical code is located, and it's even "darker" when dealing with external libraries in your code.

To provide clarity, a solution many library developers do is to **add a prefix** to the extension method names.

For example, if the library name is `StringTools`, the developer might add the library name initials as a prefix for all its functions – "st_<function name>":

```
let newString = originalString.st_
stringByRemovingHTMLEntities()
```

The "st" prefix indicates that the function is probably not part of the Swift language itself, which can be an excellent way to solve the clarity issue.

Inout Parameter

Parameters in a Swift function are passed as constants, meaning they cannot be changed.

Don't be confused between value and reference types – when a reference type is a constant, you can change one of their properties but not their actual value.

An inout parameter lets you pass a mutable parameter the function can modify.

Let's bring back again our code snippet with an inout parameter (remember, String is a value type):

```
func removeHTMLEntities(string : inout String) { }

StringUtils().removeHTMLEntities(string: &originalString)
```

Doesn't it look convenient?

Well, some developers like to make use of inout parameters in many of their functions.

An inout parameter makes the return value redundant and may look like a convenient way to easily modify an existing value.

But an inout parameter also contains some problematic issues underneath.

Functions with inout parameters have obviously side effects, and side effects are something that can reduce control in your code.

Side effects such as inout parameters become even more critical in threads when they might modify an instance value in the wrong thread.

But the good part is that you can easily avoid the inout parameter – you can just change it to a return value and assign it again to the passed parameter.

```
myString = StringUtils().getStringByRemovingHTMLEntities
(string: myString)
```

So, what is the recommendation? Many APIs contain the two ways and let the developer choose what's more convenient for him.

But anyway, my recommendation is not to give up the "return value" way.

Naming

Naming your functions and properties is a crucial part of the experience you provide for your developer (again, which is the "user," but he can also be yourself).

Naming conventions are essential regardless if they are implemented inside a library or not.

But when we design a library, it gets even more critical.

So here are some thumb rules that can help you create a great API for your package.

Clarity

"One rule to rule them all" – this one is perhaps the most important. Try to make your interface look like plain English and precisely describe your method/class/property.

Some examples:

```
func insert(index : Int) { } // not good. To where?
func insertItem(atIndex index : Int) { } // good

func updateView() { } // not good. Is it always?
func updateViewSizeIfNeeded() { } // better
```

Creating short, brevity names is important, but clarity is much more important.

So, don't be afraid of creating long method names if needed.

For example, "updateView()" doesn't mean anything – update what exactly? Content? Size? And in what cases?

This is why `updateViewSizeIfNeeded()` describes precisely what the method does and when.

Consistency

This one is important, especially if you have multiple classes in your package.

Why is consistency important? Because it makes your developer expect a particular behavior when calling one of your methods or allocating an instance for one of your classes.

Being clear in different cases doesn't mean being consistent.

For example, if in one class, you have a method named:

```
func append(item : Item)
```

and, in another class, you have a method named

```
func add(item : Item)
```

They are both clear, but this is not a consistent interface – we should use the same terms across our methods to make our interface unified, especially if our package is big.

Consistency helps your user flatten its learning curve and can ease his usage over time.

Class/Protocol Names

A class name is usually a **noun**, representing what the class does, and a protocol name is based on its methods' behavior.

When talking about **protocol naming**, we first need to understand the different protocols we have. Take a look at Table 4-1.

Table 4-1. *Different types of protocols*

Behavior	Description	Naming Convention	Example
Action enablers	Enables to perform a set of actions	Ends with "able"	Equatable
Type conversations	Enables us to convert data type to another	Ends with "Convertible"	TitleConvertible
Delegates	Enables us to give responsibility to other objects	Ends with "Delegate"	NetworkServiceDelegate

Table 4-1 is just an example of some naming conventions you can apply to protocols.

This book is not about a protocol or what kinds of protocols we have in Swift or Objective-C.

When you design an interface to be used by other developers, I recommend taking another minute or two and thinking about your protocol naming.

Unlike classes, protocol usage is far more abstract and flexible; therefore, it requires more thought to be clearer.

Method Names

We already discussed consistency and clarity. Another thing you should address when writing a method signature is its **parameters**.

As you already know, in Swift (and Objective-C), you can give names to your function arguments and make them look like a full sentence, for example:

```
func remove(itemWith name : String)
```

A quick look at the preceding function signature reveals that it's a full and clear sentence.

But now, look at what happens when we try to use this function:

```
remove(itemWith:"test")
```

Okay, "item with" what exactly? The "name" doesn't appear in the function implementation. Maybe it's an ID?

You need to remember that when using argument labels (which is the "itemWith" part), the actual argument names don't appear when calling the function itself.

To fix that, we can change the signature to something like this:

```
func remove(itemWithName name : String)
```

And the usage will be

```
remove(itemWithName:"test")
```

which is much clearer.

This also applies to the rest of the function arguments, of course:

```
func remove(itemWithName name : String, andAge age : Int)
```

```
// to use it:
remove(itemWithName: "test", andAge: 50)
```

Another thing you should consider when naming methods. Take a look at the following example:

```
func removeItemWith(name : String)
// or
func remove(itemWithName name : String)
```

In the first example, the method name is longer and includes the first parameter name ("ItemWith").

However, in the second example, the first parameter name is not part of the method name.

While this seems like a minor difference, it may be a bigger one when the number of methods in your library increases.

Let's see what happens when we add more "remove" methods:

```
func removeItemWith(name : String)
func removeTitleFrom(item : Item)
func removeAgeFrom(item : Item)

// or
func remove(itemWithName name : String)
func remove(titleFromItem item : Item)
func remove(ageFromItem item : Item)
```

Hopefully, you now see the difference. Moving the first parameter name into the parentheses creates consistency with your method's name, while they only contain the short version of the action.

And that's just logical – it is a thumb rule for you to remember – the first parameter name should be part of the first argument name and not part of the function name.

To summarize the naming part, being consistent and clear with your API is probably the best tip you can get. As long as you are consistent, whoever uses your API is going to work out just fine.

Comments

Emily, Kyle, and Joshua had a weekly meeting, discussing the following week.

"I think we should document our network library. Creating a library is an opportunity to start a technical documentation for our code," Emily said.

"I don't think it's a good idea to create a separate document for that. No one looks at documents," Kyle answered. "Feels like a waste of time."

"Maybe we can just write more comments," Joshua suggested.

Emily thought about it. Writing comments is always good, but there are plenty of ways to document your code. The problem is, as Kyle said, no one looks at documentation.

Emily didn't know that Xcode can display relevant documentation when needed as part of the code completion feature.

Rendered Documentation

Developers are not crazy about documentation – after all, we read code better than English ☺, but if there is something we hate more than reading documentation, it is to write one.

But I think that one thing we can all agree on is that providing the right documentation at the right moment is probably the most useful way to document your library.

Fortunately, many IDEs (including Xcode, of course) have a neat feature that lets you comment on your classes, methods, and properties. These comments become your documentation for your code, given automatically to the developer as part of its code auto-completion feature.

I guess we all know the function description we see during our code, as shown in Figure 4-3.

```
let array = [1,2,3,4,5]
let result = array.removeFirst|
                   M  removeFirst()
                   M  removeFirst(_ k:)
                   removeFirst() -> Int
                   Removes and returns the first element of the
                   collection.
```

Figure 4-3. *Auto-generated documentation for removeFirst array method*

Option + tapping the function name opens up even more detailed information, as you can see in Figure 4-4.

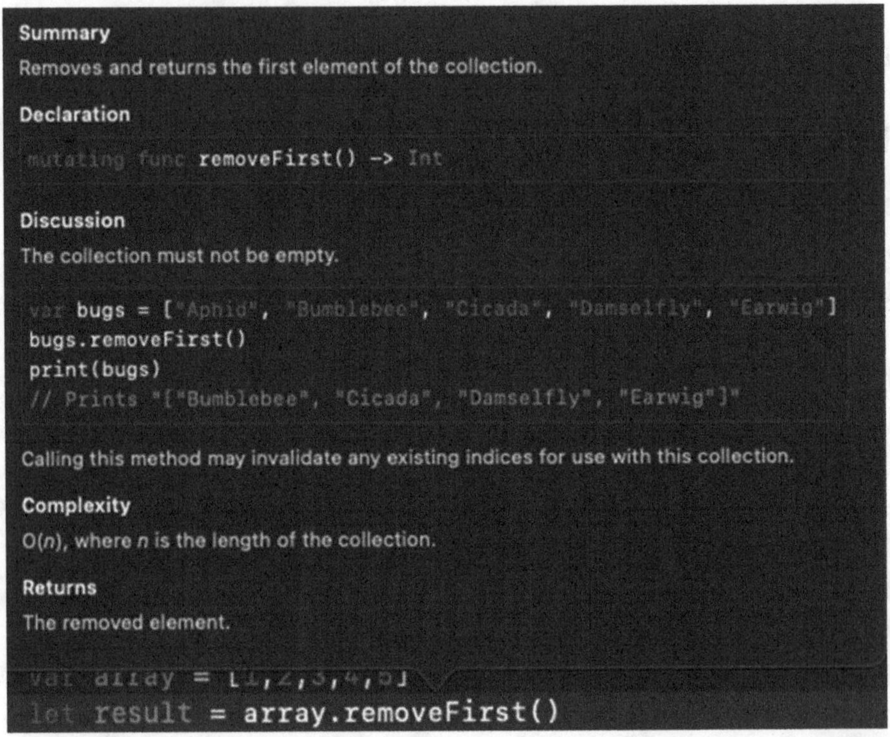

Summary
Removes and returns the first element of the collection.

Declaration

```
mutating func removeFirst() -> Int
```

Discussion
The collection must not be empty.

```
var bugs = ["Aphid", "Bumblebee", "Cicada", "Damselfly", "Earwig"]
bugs.removeFirst()
print(bugs)
// Prints "["Bumblebee", "Cicada", "Damselfly", "Earwig"]"
```

Calling this method may invalidate any existing indices for use with this collection.

Complexity
O(n), where n is the length of the collection.

Returns
The removed element.

```
var array = [1,2,3,4,5]
let result = array.removeFirst()
```

Figure 4-4. *More detailed information regarding the "removeFirst" method*

Creating documentation like that is easy and doesn't require any unique tool – it is just part of your code comments.

If we hold ⌘ and tap the function name, we can see the actual comment written and examine its markup format:

```
/// Removes and returns the first element of the
collection.
///
```

```
/// The collection must not be empty.
///
///     var bugs = ["Aphid", "Bumblebee", "Cicada",
"Damselfly", "Earwig"]
///     bugs.removeFirst()
///     print(bugs)
///     // Prints "["Bumblebee", "Cicada", "Damselfly",
"Earwig"]"
///
/// Calling this method may invalidate any existing indices
for use with this
/// collection.
///
/// - Returns: The removed element.
///
/// - Complexity: O(*n*), where *n* is the length of the
collection.
@inlinable public mutating func removeFirst() -> Element
```

Let's go over how this markup language works and how Xcode uses it
to give your developer easy-to-read documentation out of it.

The Basics

The best thing about documenting your code using a markup language is
that it is intuitive and easy.

To document a method, we just need to start a comment block above it:

```
/**

        // here goes your documentation
*/
func add(_ item : Item, toList list : [List]) { ... }
```

Unlike a regular comment block, you need to start with a /** with two stars to document.

Instead of opening a block, you can use three slashes for every comment row, just like the example in the previous section:

```
/// This is a documentation block.
/// using three slashes,
/// instead of /** - */
func add(_ item : Item, toList list : [List]) { ... }
```

Both ways are valid. The three slashes way is less convenient to use, but it is advantageous when trying to understand git commit differences.

Discussion and Summary

The comment's block is separated into **paragraphs**. Blank lines quickly do this.

Xcode automatically distinguishes between two parts – the first paragraph is part of something called **Summary**, and it appears at the top of the documentation. The other paragraphs belong to something called **Discussion**, containing all the further details, such as parameters and references.

Parameters, Returns, and Throws

Besides a summary of the function, you can also separately document the function's different parameters and return value.

Here is an example:

```
- Parameter string: The string to be modified.
```

Two things you need to know about this part:

- For Xcode (and other markup generators) to recognize these fields, you need to add a dash ("-") at the start of the row. This is true for all special fields.

- After the special field name (for instance, **Parameter**), you need to add a colon (":").

Here is an example of these fields:

```
- Parameter string: The string to be modified.

- Returns: The new modified string.

- Throws: An error in case of a failure.
```

And this is how it looks in the Xcode documentation panel whenever the cursor is placed inside the function name (Figure 4-5).

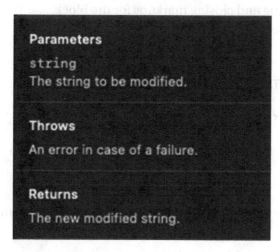

Figure 4-5. *Special fields in the Xcode documentation panel*

If you have more than one parameter, you need to add a "Parameter" field for each one of them or group them under the "Parameters" field, like this:

```
- Parameters:
    - string: The string to be modified.
    - y: The *y* component of the vector.
```

Pay attention – the **parameter/parameters** field won't work correctly if you misspelled the argument's name.

Code Blocks

Sometimes it's important to show code examples, especially at the right timing.

Sure, we can add a few code lines in the comments, but we want it to look like a code block with syntax highlighting and not just plain text.

Fortunately, it is elementary to do that. There are two ways – to **indent our code with four spaces**, and the second one is the **use of three "~" or "`"** as the opening and closing markups for the block.

Let's see that in this example:

```
/**

    Remove HTML entities from a given string.

    # Code example:

        StringUtils().remove(itemWithName: "Jason", andAge: 50)

*/
```

Now let's see how it looks in Xcode auto-generated documentation (Figure 4-6).

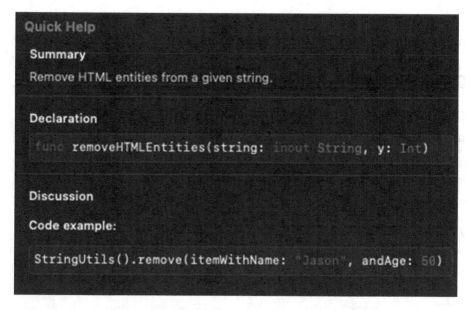

Figure 4-6. *Adding code example to our method comments*

Tip   The best timing for writing public method documentation is probably when you write unit tests. At this stage, you are familiar with the function and its parameters, and you already have some code examples from your tests.

More Special Fields

Other than the fields mentioned previously, such as Parameter and Return, there are additional particular fields you can use to document your code that are recognized by Xcode.

Here are some of them:

Precondition, Postcondition, Requires, Invariant, Complexity, Important, Warning, Author, Authors, Copyright, Date, SeeAlso, Since, Version, Attention, Bug, Experiment, Note, Remark, ToDo

All the preceding field titles are rendered as bold in the quick help and fully recognized in different documentation generators you can use.

Document Classes, Structs, and Enum

Documenting your code using comments doesn't have to end with only methods – you can also document your classes, structures, and enums.

There is no special magic here – you document classes precisely the way you do it for functions.

Take a look at this:

```
/**
This class handles many string functionality.

Here are some code examples
~~~
var originalString = "Hello. <br> This is a string with
<b>HTML</b> entities"
StringUtils().removeHTMLEntities(string: &originalString, y: 5)
~~~
*/
class StringUtils {

    /// This is a shared singleton to manage string states.
    static let shared = StringUtils()
```

Writing the comments just above your classes provides Xcode the ability to render the documentation and display it when needed. See Figure 4-7.

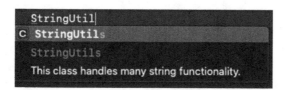

Figure 4-7. *Class documentation displayed in auto-completion Xcode feature*

Summary

In this chapter, we've learned all about package design and linking.

In the next chapter, you'll learn how packages work together using the dependencies mechanism and how to do that without creating significant constraints.

CHAPTER 5

All About Dependencies

If you don't actively fight for simplicity in software, complexity will win...and it will suck.

—Henry Joreteg

In the previous chapter, we learned how to design great packages. Now, we need to learn how to connect packages, not only in a technical way but also in the right way.

In this chapter, we will learn

- What "code coupling" is

- What types of code coupling we have and why it matters

- How to create all kinds of dependencies' requirements, including version, revisions, and branch based

- How to reduce coupling level to make our project more flexible

© Avi Tsadok 2021
A. Tsadok, *Mastering Swift Package Manager*,
https://doi.org/10.1007/978-1-4842-7049-3_5

A Utils Package

Kyle was doing a code review for Joshua on the new network package he wrote, and then he saw something weird.

He went to Joshua's desk to discuss it with him.

"Hey, Joshua, I saw that you used some functions we already have in our Utils class. Why did you copy them into the package? It's code duplication."

For developers, especially professional developers like Kyle, saying "code duplication" sounds a profanity.

"I had no choice," Joshua defended himself. "There is no way for a package to use code from the project. Otherwise, what's the point?"

Joshua was right. He had to duplicate the code and insert it into the package to use it.

"So why don't we create a 'Utils Package' and share it both with our project and the network package?", Kyle suggested.

"That's a great idea!", Joshua answered, "But I don't know how to do it... and it may cause something I've learned in college, called 'code coupling,' which I'm not sure it's a positive thing. Let me check it!"

Code Coupling

First, let's understand what code coupling is.

Code coupling is the level of connection between two software components.

It is widespread to always think about coupling as "one class has a reference to another class," but the truth is that code coupling is much more than that.

The more abstract way to describe code coupling is **"Is changing one class code mean I need to change another class?"**

I general, we want the answer to the preceding question to be "no" in most cases.

Why Code Coupling Matters?

Code coupling levels are considered to be (another) indication of code quality you should address.

When discussing "pure functions," we like to talk about side effects your function might have – well, high code coupling means that every code change may have side effects of changes you need to do in other areas of your code.

And this influences your ability to make changes to your code, fix bugs, and refactor and even understand your app architecture and design patterns.

Think of code coupling as constraints and contracts you unintentionally add to your codebase.

We cannot wholly avoid code coupling in our app. In the end, your classes need to work with each other somehow. Otherwise, it's not an app but rather a set of classes.

But we can reduce the number of classes connected and reduce the coupling level in those already being connected.

And why are we discussing code coupling now? Because coupling is the essence of building a good Swift Package. The way your library fits into your app or any other app relies on how it couples with your project or other libraries as well.

Sometimes, high coupling means that in some projects, it can be impossible to use your package.

Fortunately, we can solve many of these issues efficiently using some basic techniques.

To do that, we need to deep dive into what coupling exactly means.

Types of Coupling

If we follow the code coupling definition mentioned earlier ("changing one class, meaning changing another one"), we can see that code coupling is more than just references between classes.

There are more ways classes may relate to each other, even without holding a direct reference.

Structural Dependencies

Structural dependencies are the "classic" dependencies we know. It mostly means a "direct connection between classes or components."

For example, when a class calls another class method, it's a structural dependency.

Structural dependency is the most frequently used dependency, and therefore, it's the easier one to locate, manage, and handle.

In structural dependency, it is accepted to distinguish between three types of dependencies – extended/inheritance, aggregates, and usage.

Inheritance

Inheritance is probably one of the most coupled design patterns that exist. It's practically a pure definition of code coupling – **every change** in the base class influences its subclasses (unless mentioned otherwise), and this operation is done recursively.

Now, let's take it back to the world of Swift Packages – if Package A relies on Package B and one of A's classes inheritance from one of B's classes, we have just created too tight coupling between our modules. You should already understand why this kind of coupling is not recommended and probably will cause future issues.

To understand how we can avoid that, we need to know **why** we had to use inheritance.

In most cases, **there are two main reasons** why most developers use inheritance (except for the fact that it's the first thing we learn in OOP).

The first reason is that we need the two classes to have the **same interface**, and the second is because we need them to have the **same implementation**.

To fill both needs, we can use other design patterns with a lower coupling level. For instance, to share interfaces, we can use **protocols**, and to share implementation, we can use **object composition**.

In other words, we need a good reason for an inheritance, especially between packages. In most cases, we can bypass it with different techniques.

Aggregation

Another way classes can be coupled is **aggregation**. Aggregation is a type of **composition** where one class uses another class and has an instance variable of the latest, for instance:

```
import EmployeePackage

class Team {
    var employees = [EmployeePackage.Employee]()
}
```

We can see that Team is coupled with Employee just by having a reference.

I also emphasize this can happen when importing a package.

Now, importing the EmployeePackage to define the employees variable is legit.

But these two classes are now coupled and tight with each other. Replacing the Employee with another class can be a hassle, and if the Employee interface changes in the future, you can expect many code modifications to do.

Fortunately, there is a simple way to decrease the coupling level in this case – by using a protocol and extending the Employee class.

This is how it's done:

```
protocol EmployeeProtocol {
    var name : String { get }
}
extension Employee : EmployeeProtocol {

    var name : String {
        return self.firstName + " " + self.lastName
    }

}


class Team {

    var employees = [EmployeeProtocol]()
}
```

By defining an EmployeeProtocol, we can decouple the class Team from the EmployeePackage and do the coupling in only one location – the Employee protocol implementation code.

Look at Figure 5-1.

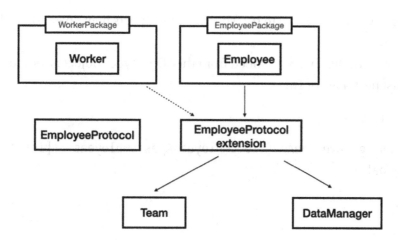

Figure 5-1. *Use protocol to decouple your code from your package*

In Figure 5-1, we can see exactly how it works – by using protocols, and we can create a system that is agnostic to changes.

Usage

In the "usage" coupling type, one class usually has a method with a parameter based on another class. This one is considered to be a more "light" coupling:

```
import EmployeePackage

class Team {

    func getAvarageAge(fromEmployees employees :
    [EmployeePackage.Employee]) -> Float {

    }
}
```

In the preceding example, Team doesn't have a reference to Employee, but one of its methods does, in its parameter.

One way to avoid it is to try "shaving" the objects being passed to what we need.

For example, if what we need from the "Employee" object is its age, we can just pass a list of `Int`:

```
class Team {

    func getAverageAge(fromEmployeesAges employees : [Int]) ->
    Float {

    }
}
```

In this way, we can even skip the `import EmployeePackage` line and make another successful decoupling.

If it's impossible to do that, we can go back to the technique we discussed earlier and pass a protocol the original object can conform to.

Both ways are legit to reduce the coupling level in our code.

Fan-Out Similarity

Structural coupling is a **direct coupling**. It is easy to identify and solve.

But not all coupling types are direct, and these are harder to understand or measure.

Indirect coupling does not always mean something, but it can be a "code smell," indicating this is something we need to investigate.

One of those types is called "Fan-Out Similarity," and it is based on structural metrics called "**Fan-Out**" and "**Fan-In**."

Fan-Out and Fan-In are two ways to describe the complexity between modules and classes.

Fan-Out – The number of modules called by a given module

Fan-In – The number of modules that call a given module

What's more interesting for us, in this case, is Fan-Out. The reason for that is that the list of connected modules in Fan-Out represents a particular functionality. If we find two (or more) modules with the same list of modules, it might indicate a similar functionality.

Look at Figure 5-2.

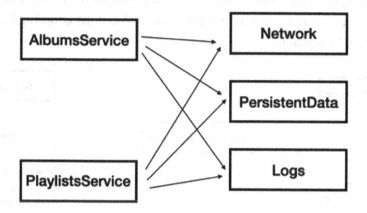

Figure 5-2. *Fan-Out Similarity demonstrated*

In Figure 5-2, we can see the two modules, AlbumsService and PlaylistsService, without a direct connection between them. But we can also see that both call to a similar set of components – Network, PersistentData, and Logs.

The higher the number of modules in this shared set, the higher the chances that both modules have similar functionality.

And this is an interesting perspective – if two modules have similar functionality, what does it mean about SoC (separation of concerns)? And what does it mean about future changes in these modules?

After a second look at Figure 5-2, we can conclude that both AlbumsService and PlaylistsService do some network calls and then save the data to the local persistent store. They probably function the same, so any change we do in this **working pattern**, most chances, influences both of them.

As I mentioned earlier, Fan-Out Similarity is mostly a "code smell." It doesn't mean we have a problem or even a coupling situation, but it means we need to look after it.

Suppose we have several modules/classes coupled because of a Fan-Out Similarity, and because of that, we found a similar working pattern. In that case, this is a chance for us to create another abstract layer that encapsulates this pattern and, by definition, reduces the coupling level.

Look at Figure 5-3.

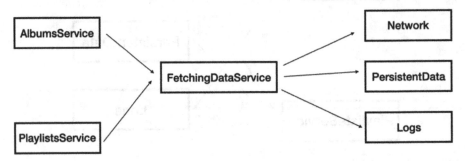

Figure 5-3. *Adding a working layer to reduce coupling level*

In Figure 5-3, we can see that AlbumsService and PlaylistsService now have low Fan-Out Similarity while referencing only one component instead of three.

Fan-Out Similarity with Inheritance

Fan-Out Similarity is relevant not only when calling other modules or classes but also with **inheritance**.

If two classes inherit from the same superclass, they are, in fact, indirectly coupled.

Now, we've discussed earlier inheritance and found two ways to avoid it – a composition and a protocol. These solutions are relevant here as well.

In previous chapters, we discussed the different access levels Swift has. If you recall, we talked about open/public. Access level of the type open allows the developer to subclass and override the marked class, method, or variable.

Now that we add the coupling consideration into our decision, we understand why marking a class as open has to be intentional.

In general, raising the access level and giving the developer more access mean increasing the chances of a coupled code, so this should be done carefully and well thought.

Logical Coupling

Logical coupling is another code smell we have in our code, and it's another determination of how two modules can be coupled even without a direct reference.

Logical coupling, also known as **evolutionary coupling**, is when two modules code changes and modify **together**.

There are plenty of examples of that. One classic example could be when we work on **permissions handling**. If we change how we handle user permissions on one area of the code, it could also mean we need to change it on different code areas simultaneously.

In fact, any broadside change or feature can lead to a logical coupling.

Remember, if code changes in one module frequently mean code changes in another module, it may point out some coupling level.

If we detect such coupling, we can try to understand the reason for that. For example, one reason could be **duplicate code**. Creating another component to encapsulate this code can be the right solution for that.

Another reason might indicate we have an issue with the **SoC (separation of concerns)** principle. If we have multiple components dealing with the same responsibility, it could be a case where we need to reconsider how we separated our code and what design patterns we need to use.

It is all circling the same issue at the bottom line – duplicate code patterns that we can encapsulate to another class or component.

Dependencies Between Packages

After we've learned what coupling is, maybe it's time to start creating some of our own.

Swift Package Manager, just like any other dependencies' manager, can manage dependencies between packages.

As I said in one of the earlier chapters, the process of resolving packages is a **recursive** one and is done solely by the package manager itself.

A package cannot be compiled unless all of its dependencies were resolved. So, one thing to take into account – dependencies are literally creating constraints in your project.

We shouldn't become addicted to adding more and more dependencies if we don't have to.

Remembering from previous chapters, some packages require a minimum version, and others require a specific platform.

Any dependency you add to your manifest file may limit you in the future using your package in new projects.

To define a new dependency, we use the package manifest file – `Package.swift`.

A Version-Based Requirement

First, what is a "version"? If you recall, we haven't seen any "version" attribute in the package manifest.

When dealing with packages that are part of a git repository, the version is determined by the **git repository tag value**.

For example, if you committed some new code to your package and created a tag 1.0.0, it means that your package version is, well, 1.0.0.

Now, the version convention is part of something called a "semantic versioning standard" – so here are some important words about it.

Semantic Versioning Standard

It is important to remember that unlike app versioning, which is mainly semantic and sometimes is part of marketing efforts, package versioning has a technical meaning.

You need to remember that managing a package means managing an API – there are issues such as interface changes, capabilities, backward compatibility, and more.

The semantic versioning standard is built out of three elements – major, minor, and patch (or "hotfix").

In version 2.5.1, 2 is the major version, 5 is the minor version, and 1 is the hotfix.

A major version – When we make a change to the API and break the backward compatibility.

A minor version – Add more functionality and capabilities, but we don't break the backward compatibility.

Hotfix – Add bug fixes without new capabilities or breaking backward compatibility.

Keeping the semantic versioning standard helps us create a dependency based on versions.

Control Our Dependencies' Update

By default, Swift Package Manager tries to update our dependencies to the latest version that satisfies our requirements.

Based on what was written in the previous section, we know that major versions might break backward compatibility.

Swift Package Manager's behavior is to update our dependencies to the **latest minor version**, which requires us to mention a major version in our requirements explicitly.

Let's look at some code examples.

To add a dependency, from a specific version:

```
dependencies: [
        .package(url: "https://mastering-swift-package.com/
        package.git", from : "4.0.0"),
    ],
```

The preceding code will update our dependency to additional "4.x.x" versions, for example, 4.1.0 or 4.2.0, up until the next major version, which is 5.0.0 (the 5.0.0 version is not included).

This is part of why keeping the logic behind the version convention is so essential – Swift Package Manager's goal is to keep the code updated with bug fixes but without breaking the backward compatibility.

In addition to updating a dependency from a specific version, we can update dependencies within a certain range:

```
        .package(url: "https://mastering-swift-package.com/
        package.git", "4.0.0"..."4.5.0"),
```

Or

```
        .package(url: "https://mastering-swift-package.com/
        package.git", "4.0.0"..<"4.5.0"),
```

The latest means "updating the dependency from version 4.0.0 to the latest version below 4.5.0."

If you want to lock the dependency to a specific version, you can use exact to do that:

```
dependencies: [
    .package(url: "https://mastering-swift-package.com/
    package.git", .exact("4.5.0")),
],
```

Aside from version-based requirements, there are more ways to lock our dependencies to a specific state, such as a branch or even a particular revision.

Branch-/Commit-Based Requirement

Limiting your dependencies' updates to a specific version or a range of versions is probably the most common way to handle your dependencies.

A version-based requirement is suitable for cases when your dependencies are in production and get updated rapidly.

However, when we are in the development stage of the dependency package, a version-based requirement might cause headaches.

For example, if we checked out to a specific branch during development, we want to work with **that specific branch** without handling versioning.

Fortunately, Swift Package Manager provides us a way to work with a specific branch:

```
dependencies: [
    .package(url: "https://mastering-swift-package.com/
    package.git", .branch("master")),
],
```

Even though working with a specific branch is great, it is also "dangerous." Branches receive new updates over time, and those can break our integration. In the development stage, it is acceptable, but in production code, it is a problem.

So, another way to solve that is to lock our dependency to **a specific git commit**:

```
dependencies: [
    .package(url: "https://mastering-swift-package.com/
    package.git", .revision("23cde90b29bb2a0cf02dfee9fe45e7
    a5c36ec7b4")),
],
```

Creating a dependency by a revision ensures that our code cannot break in the future from package updates and versions, but on the other hand, it will never get any bug fixes or new features.

A Local Dependency

Another way to add a dependency would be pointing to a local Swift Package.

Working with a local dependency is very similar to working with remote dependency:

```
dependencies: [
    .package(url: "~/Code/LocalPackage/", from : "1.0.0"),
],
```

Looking at the preceding code, you probably noticed two interesting issues.

First, I used an **absolute path** to the package location. Of course, this is not something I recommend. Using an absolute path will work most of the time on your local machine, but it will break once it goes out to a CI/CD machine or a different developer.

The recommended way is to use a **relative path**:

```
dependencies: [
    .package(url: "../LocalPackage/", from : "1.0.0"),
],
```

And, of course, make sure `LocalPackage` is located in the right place. This is something we are going to learn in one of the next chapters.

The second issue is the versioning. Even if we maintain a local package, it's still an option to create a specific git repository just for that.

Everything that we've learned before about dependency requirements – versioning, branches, and revisions – is relevant to local dependencies as well.

To simplify the integration, we can add the local dependency while ignoring any requirements:

```
dependencies: [
    .package(url: "../LocalPackage/"),
],
```

So, we understand now how to define a package dependency. But another place we can define a dependency is in our project.

Project's Remote Dependencies

Besides creating local Swift Packages and integrating them with our project, we can easily connect our project to a remote package.

In fact, this is one of the main goals of Swift Package Manager – to create a package and share it with other developers.

To integrate a Swift Package located in a remote git repository, go to the File menu in Xcode 11 and then Swift Packages ➤ Add Package Dependency....

There are two ways of adding a remote Swift Package. The first one is to search using your GitHub account, and the second is to provide the package full URL path.

If no GitHub (or Bitbucket, for that matter) account is linked to your Xcode, you'll see the following message when trying to add a remote package (Figure 5-4).

Figure 5-4. *Adding a package dependency without a git account*

In this case, you can still enter the full package URL.

On the other hand, if you have a git account registered in Xcode, you'll see the list of packages that exist in your account (Figure 5-5).

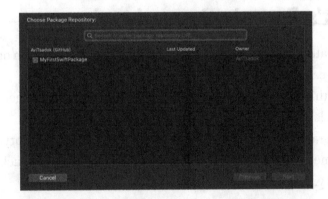

Figure 5-5. *List of Swift Packages in your git account*

Unlike what you see in Figure 5-5, when you have a git account registered, you can also search for a public Swift Package. For example, in Figure 5-6, you can see the search results for FMDB Swift Package.

Figure 5-6. *Swift Package search results in Xcode 12*

Before moving forward and linking the package, you can retrieve more details by selecting the package in the search results. A short description, including the number of forks, starred, and a link to the readme file, will appear on the window's bottom.

Selecting and pressing the "Next" button takes us to the package options dialog, which lets us configure the package updating mechanism, similar to what we have in our Package manifest file. Look at Figure 5-7.

Figure 5-7. *Package options dialog*

In Figure 5-7, we can see a nice UI representation of the version updating locking method we learned earlier. Pressing "Next" starts the resolving and fetching process (Figure 5-8).

Figure 5-8. *Resolving and fetching package process*

After resolving, we can see the new package in our project navigator (Figure 5-9).

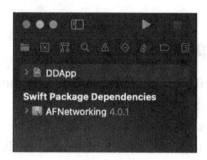

Figure 5-9. *The new package in the project navigator pane*

Our package in the navigator is now connected to the project and becomes one of its dependencies.

It is essential to know that the fact that we see the package in our project navigator doesn't mean that its files are part of the project. These files were downloaded to the derived data folder and are managed solely by Xcode.

Some Best Practices About Dependencies

On one side, we see how easy it is to add dependencies to our project. On the other side, we understand now how it can make things more complicated.

Code coupling is a major issue, especially in big projects that have to be maintained over time.

So, the first and primary rule here is **avoid dependencies if possible**.

It doesn't mean we shouldn't have any dependencies in our project. But with every dependency you add, you need to consider the constraints it brings with it.

We can most of the time bypass dependencies between packages by using different design patterns, and we can decrease the coupling level significantly.

Reducing Coupling Level

It is easy to think that if one library needs to use another library's services, it means they are tightly coupled.

This by any means doesn't have to be the case.

For example, let's take the case where a network client library needs to use a logging library.

The naïve approach for that is to make the logging library a dependency of the network client. Still, it means that every project or a library that wants to make use of the network library will have to support the logging library as well.

This approach has ways to bypass it. One of them is dependency injection.

Dependency Injection

As I said earlier, we can solve many of these problems using simple design patterns. One of the design patterns we can use is dependency injection, based on the network client library protocol.

Take a look at the following code:

```
protocol LoggerProtocol {

    func logInfo(str : String, level : Int)
    func logError(str : String, level : Int)
}
```

```
class NetworkClient {

    let logger : LoggerProtocol

    init(logger : LoggerProtocol) {
        self.logger = logger
    }
}
extension Logger : LoggerProtocol {

}
```

With dependency injection, we initialize the network client using any class that conforms to LoggerProtocol. The implementation of LoggerProtocol is done in the project easily, and this means that NetworkClient can work with any instance that can write logs (it doesn't have to be even a logging library). The connections and wiring are all made in the project itself.

We can see the difference in Figure 5-10.

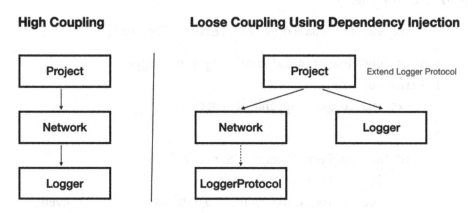

Figure 5-10. *How to loosen coupling using dependency injection and protocols*

We can also use dependency injection when we want to keep our library "clean" from dependencies and keep only the necessary logic while integrating other services or libraries.

For example, we can retake our logger example. We know that logging is done by various libraries, each one of them does it a little bit differently. In this case, we want to have one library to be the only access point for logging in to our app.

But we don't want it to be dependent on the other third-party libraries. We want to **inject them** into our library.

In the following code snippet, we solved just that. Creating a protocol named ExternalLogger allows us to subscribe to any logging library to our Logger library very easily, without coupling our code.

```
public protocol ExternalLogger : class{
    var name : String { get }
    func logEvent(event : String)
}

public class Logger {

    private var externalLoggers = [ExternalLogger]()

    public func subscribeExternalLogger(newLogger :
    ExternalLogger) {
        externalLoggers.append(newLogger)
    }

    public func logEvent(event : String) {
        for logger in externalLoggers {
            logger.logEvent(event: logger.name + ": " + event)
        }
    }
}
```

In Figure 5-11, we can see how our library tree is flat and how we can use the project as a coordinator to inject different third-party libraries to our logger library, which is very thin and light.

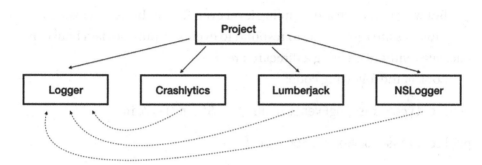

Figure 5-11. *Inject third-party libraries to the logger library*

This design pattern not only reduces coupling level but also solves other issues we might have with dependencies.

One of these issues is package requirements.

If you remember, in one of the first chapters, we discussed how requirements and dependencies work together.

We know that if a package requires a specific platform or a minimum version, it means that all the packages that depended on that package **need at least** the same requirements.

Today, there is no option to define a package dependency as "optional," and that fact makes us rethink how to connect our packages in a useful way.

If we look again at our Logger package, we know that some of the third-party loggers attached to it don't work on specific platforms.

For example, Crashlytics doesn't work on watchOS. It means that when we set up Logger on our Apple Watch extension, we can **define precisely what loggers are injected** into our package and, by that, solve the issue of the minimum requirement.

Using Closures

We saw that the combination of dependency injection and protocols is excellent for reducing the coupling level.

But we can reduce the coupling level even further by using closures.

Closures are a great way to respond to events or provide data between packages without creating a direct reference.

Look at the following code:

```
public typealias LogEventClosure = (String)->Void

public class Logger : NSObject {

    public var reportLogEvent : LogEventClosure?

    public func logEvent(event : String) {
        reportLogEvent?(event)
    }
}

var logger = Logger()
logger.reportLogEvent = { event in

    // report 'event' in any third party logger in this closure.
}
```

Implementing closures also creates a more testable code, but in some way, it transfers some of the logic to the closure itself.

The Responsibility Is on the App

We can see now that we have two ways to connect between packages – the first is using the Swift Package, dependency manager. The other is using dependency injection or closures.

In the second way, the coupling level is much lower.

But it also requires the app to link between them and even deal with some of the logic itself.

As always, it's a trade-off we, as developers, always need to consider.

Summary

In this chapter, we covered everything we need to know about dependencies.

As an infrastructure for that, we've learned what code coupling is and what types of coupling we have.

We've learned how to create a package dependency and a project dependency.

We also learned some techniques to reduce the coupling level and provide more flexibility to our project architecture.

In the next chapter, we will learn how to take advantage of Swift Package Manager to share code not only within our project but also with other developers and with other projects.

CHAPTER 6

And Sharing for All

There is an easy way and a hard way. The hard part is finding the easy way.

—Anonymous

Emily called Kyle and Joshua for a short discussion.

"Ok, remember our second app, 'Weather for all'? The back-end team doesn't want to keep maintaining two servers, and they asked us to unify our requests to the same endpoints."

"Now that we have the network Swift Package, we can duplicate it and add it to the project. Few hours and we all set," Kyle suggested.

Emily didn't like the idea: "But that's code duplication. What's the point of having a Swift Package if, eventually, we can't share it?"

"Maybe we can share it," Joshua said. "Maybe we can upload it to git in a separated repository and link it to both our apps."

"It's a good idea," Emily said. "But that means exposing, because we'll have to make it public, no?"

"I don't know," Joshua answered. "It's a good question. I need to search a little bit."

The problem our iOS team is facing is a common one. We are always saying code sharing is essential, and Swift Package is a great way to share code. But how exactly do we do it? And how do we handle security?

© Avi Tsadok 2021
A. Tsadok, *Mastering Swift Package Manager*,
https://doi.org/10.1007/978-1-4842-7049-3_6

In this chapter, we'll learn about

- How to share code using a public git repository

- How to handle versioning when we have several projects

- How to create a good Readme.md file

- How to connect to a Swift Package, hosted in a private git repository, using personal access token and SSH

- What a Monorepo is and what its pros and cons are

Sharing Options

When we had one project, it was easy. We just created some local packages in our project and linked them easily.

If you remember, we can even use a relative path to create dependencies between our packages (if needed, of course), and everything seems to be simple.

But we know that one of Swift Packages' benefits is the ability to share and reuse code not only within our project and targets but also between projects, between developers, and even with developers around the world.

But as simple as it sounds, just uploading the package to a git repository and connecting it, in reality, it may come with a cost of complexity and security issues.

There are several techniques of sharing your package between your projects, with many pros and cons, and we'll go over them in this chapter.

Sharing Using a Public Git Repo

Uploading your package to a public git repo is one of the simplest ways of dealing with sharing your Swift Package.

However, there are several things you need to be aware of with this approach.

There Is No Support for Multipackage Repositories

As of this writing, a git repository can only have one Swift Package, meaning you need to create a repository for each Swift Package you want to share.

While it may sound obvious, when we talked about taking our existing app and breaking it up into packages, it means that for every package, you need to

- Create a local package containing files from your project

- Connect the local package and integrate your app to see that everything is working as it should

- Create a git repository and upload the files to git

- Connect the app to the git repository

So, while setting up remote Swift Packages may sound like a big hassle, it gives you the ability to maintain each package separately, with different developers and different access controls.

Putting your Swift Packages on public repositories gives you another interesting opportunity – make some of your logic an open source library. An open source library can let other developers worldwide help you maintain your code without exposing them to other parts of your app.

Versioning

Versioning is a pain point, relevant not only for Swift Packages but also for any external library you implement in your project.

The first stage of writing a library and adding it to your project is relatively easy. It is similar to adding a new set of classes to your app.

Once your library is shared across multiple projects, we assume that it is not standing still and evolves based on project requirements over time.

Remember that a first-party library is not a classic product – we (that is to say, an app) demand modifications or add-ons, and then we implement them into our library.

The described process may cause us backward compatibility with other apps and projects depending on that library.

The issue gets even worse when different projects **and even other libraries** are dependent on that particular library we just changed.

The fact that we manage each library independently, in its git repository, and potentially with many developers (since it's public) makes the backward compatibility problem a real issue we need to deal with.

Remember Semantic Versioning Standard?

If you remember from the previous chapter, semantic versioning standard aims to address precisely that.

When your dependencies' management is done remotely, you need to keep in mind the next two rules:

- Every dependency **requirement needs to be defined according to its life cycle** stage. After the initial library development is finished, the worst thing you can do is lock the dependency to a particular git branch, particularly the main branch. Sticking to a branch may cause incompatible updates in the future that may cause your app or your library to break.

– The versioning process needs to be **according to semantic versioning standard**. While it sounds obvious to you, it doesn't mean it is clear for the other developers that work on that library, especially when it is a public one. This should be taken into consideration when doing code reviews and pull requests.

Keeping the versioning rules on both sides (the dependency requirement definition and the library itself) improves your integrations' stability from breaking.

Testing

Semantic versioning standard is a great way to sustain backward compatibility – on a paper.

In reality, code breaks even without public interface changes, just because developers create bugs and change behaviors, sometimes even without being aware of them.

Semantic versioning standard is just part of the solution.

Also, another critical tool we can use to catch issues is testing.

We haven't discussed testing just yet, but testing is a primary weapon when fighting backward compatibility issues.

When talking about testing in this context, we refer to two types of testing – unit and integration tests.

In short, unit tests aim to catch certain use cases of the library functions with specific parameters, and integration tests' goal is to see how your libraries work together.

Even though we'll discuss testing in the next chapter, I want to clear up something in terms of backward compatibility.

One of the test's primary goals is to catch any regressions in your code. In this case, bugs may be created due to code changes in the library itself or one of the library dependencies.

Remember that unit tests (and especially integration tests) are not supposed to be written without context. You should always create your tests based on user stories or, in this case, based on **how the client (another library or an app) uses your package**.

For example, if your app calls one of your package functions with certain parameters and expects a specific result, you should write a test covering **just that**. Sure, it is useful to cover edge case scenarios, but covering particular use cases ensures your code won't break in the future.

When talking about Swift Packages, integration tests become even more critical. If your package is dependent on other packages, integration tests ensure this dependency fulfills the required behavior. Integration tests become even more critical when discussing open source packages with the nature of receiving code updates supposed to fill different projects' demands.

Remember, Public Is Public

Some of our packages contain sensitive information we don't want to expose to the world.

Some of them are not even relevant to other developers around the world.

This means that making some of our code an open source project is not always what we want, so what do we do?

In previous chapters, we learned how to decouple modules in our code and use different design patterns to do it.

The same approach can be used in this case to take out some private information and then enjoy the benefits of sharing your code.

The leading principle here (again) is SoC ("**s**eparation **o**f **c**oncerns") – separating the private information from the package itself lets you put the package on a public repository in the future.

Not only can separating private information help you make your package public, but it can also make it more reusable and testable.

For instance, let's take our networking package. Instead of putting the list of endpoints inside the package, we can separate them into a different file hosted by the app. Take a look at Figure 6-1.

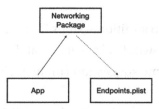

Figure 6-1. *Separate endpoints list from the networking package*

The Endpoints.plist contains all the endpoints and their HTTP request methods (Figure 6-2).

Key	Type	Value
⌄ Root	Dictionary	(2 items)
⌄ sync	Dictionary	(2 items)
method	String	https://www.server.com/sync/
url	String	POST
⌄ login	Dictionary	(2 items)
url	String	https://www.server.com/login/
method	String	POST

Figure 6-2. *Endpoints.plist file*

Now, this is an example of how to take a private package and make it public.

The conversion to a public repository reduces complexity and can give you additional benefits of better design and faster bug fixes.

Distribute Your Package

In general, the fact that your package repository is public and not private means it is already available for others to clone and integrate it into their projects.

There is no need to do additional steps for that to happen.

There is no "official" Swift Package index at the time of this writing, even though there are some suggestions in the Swift developer's community to create one.

Searching from Xcode for a Swift Package will find your package (or other public packages) as long as it is public. But a real, official index does not yet exist.

However, there are some alternative indexes where you can find many Swift Packages to use. The most famous one is `https://swiftpackageindex.com`, containing thousands of public Swift Packages for you to use.

It has a great search engine and full detailed information for each package. I recommend you add your package to that index or any other index, for that matter.

Readme.md File

We didn't talk about the `Readme.md` file yet, and perhaps now is the time for that.

There are three different aspects we document our package – the first is comments, which provide relevant documentation while coding, and we discussed that in previous chapters. The second is unit tests that other than making sure our package performs as expected are part of the documentation.

The third is the `Readme.md` file.

The `Readme.md` file is the first file git hosting services show when a developer entered the repository.

Readme.me file acts as a "manual" and contains useful package information, such as

- Package goal

- Installation details

- Setup steps

- Usage

- Different notes

The Readme.md file is important in private repositories as well, but in public repositories, it is critical documentation.

Remember that your package may contain many Swift files. Documenting every public interface using comments is excellent, but it doesn't answer the developer question "What is the 'main' file?"

In other words, the one question every Readme.md file should answer is "How do I start?"

As I said, even in private packages, that information can be important while we share it with other developers in our team or even forget that ourselves.

Readme.md File Location and Formatting

The Readme.md file should be located in the root folder of your package, but don't worry about that – when creating a new Swift Package, a Readme.md file is automatically generated for you.

In Figure 6-3, you can see part of the Readme.md file of FMDB Swift Package.

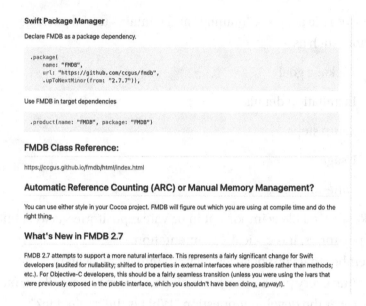

Swift Package Manager

Declare FMDB as a package dependency.

```
.package(
    name: "FMDB",
    url: "https://github.com/ccgus/fmdb",
    .upToNextMinor(from: "2.7.7")),
```

Use FMDB in target dependencies

```
.product(name: "FMDB", package: "FMDB")
```

FMDB Class Reference:

https://ccgus.github.io/fmdb/html/index.html

Automatic Reference Counting (ARC) or Manual Memory Management?

You can use either style in your Cocoa project. FMDB will figure out which you are using at compile time and do the right thing.

What's New in FMDB 2.7

FMDB 2.7 attempts to support a more natural interface. This represents a fairly significant change for Swift developers (audited for nullability; shifted to properties in external interfaces where possible rather than methods; etc.). For Objective-C developers, this should be a fairly seamless transition (unless you were using the ivars that were previously exposed in the public interface, which you shouldn't have been doing, anyway!).

Figure 6-3. *FMDB Readme.md file*

As you can see from Figure 6-3, the Readme.md file is not a plain text document. The "md" extension refers to "**MarkD**own," and it is elementary to create a well rich, documented file for your library.

Readme.md Markdown Formatting

The Readme.md markdown formatting is probably one of the most straightforward formats that exist.

Some basic rules:

One hash mark (#) at the beginning of the sentence produces a title.

Adding more hash marks ("##", "###") **adds headers in different sizes** correspondingly.

A sequence of three apostrophes (```) is used to **start a code snippet**, and another series of three apostrophes are used to close the code snippet.

Adding a link is done using the following format: [<Displayed name>] (URL).

For example:

`[Apple Inc](www.apple.com)`

You can also make the text richer:

Bold – **This is bold text** (**This is bold text**)

Italic – *Italic text* (*Italic text*)

Strikethrough – ~~This is a strikethrough text~~ (~~This is a strikethrough text~~)

Creating lists – You can use the same symbols you generally use to create lists, such as -, a digit, or *.

You can even insert images and GIF animations to your `Readme.md` file quite easily by using the link formatting I mentioned previously.

Figure 6-4 shows an example of a `Readme.md` source file and how it looks on GitHub.

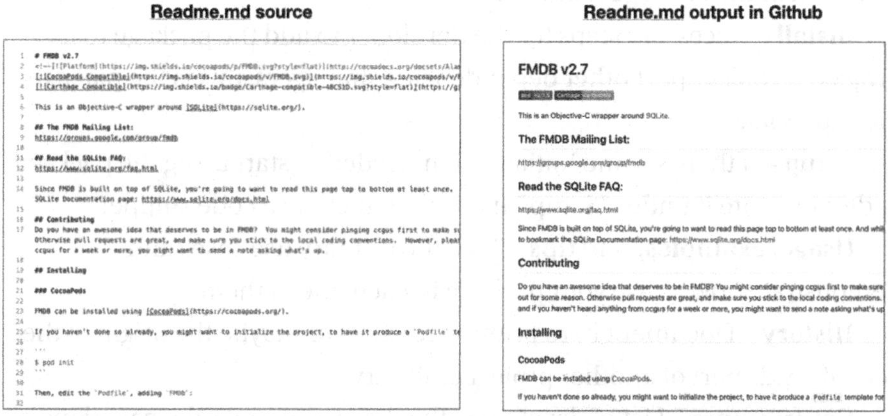

Figure 6-4. *FMDB Readme.md file – source vs. output in GitHub*

Unlike HTML, the markup language used in `Readme.md` files is straightforward and clear even in the source version.

Readme.md Best Practices

The Readme.md formatting is not the most crucial part of the file, but rather its content.

Most Readme.md files are structured into sections, describing the different package's areas implementation and usage.

Here are some of the sections that are recommended to be included in your Readme.md file:

Overview – Describing in short what the package does and what it aims to solve.

What's new? – Describe what's new in the latest release. Update this section with every release.

Requirements – Usually what platforms and minimum versions are required for the package to be installed. This can be corresponding to what is written in the Package.swift file.

Install – Necessary steps for the developer to add the package to its project. If you support other dependencies' managers, this is the place to mention that.

Setup – If there's some initialization needed to start using the package code, you write it under "Setup." It is best to include a code snippet.

Usage, examples, and tips – Take the primary use cases and demonstrate how to use your package in each one of them.

History – Document here primary releases or maybe the origin of the code if it was part of another project or library.

Contributors – List of developers that have a central role in working on the library.

Support and bugs – What to do in case of a problem? How to open an issue?

You don't have to add all the preceding sections, but this list can give you a good picture of how Readme.md files are built and what types of information are expected to be included.

Adding Pictures and Animations

Another good way to demonstrate your package, which many developers ignore, is visual explanations.

In case your package deals with UI elements, you can add images to your Readme.md files to show how it performs. Not only that, but you can also add GIF animations to show the UI behavior.

Besides "eye-catching," adding visual content also helps you explain what your package does better than any words.

To add images or GIF animations, you can use the markdown formatting rules mentioned previously.

Private Git Repository

There are cases when exposing our Swift Packages to the public is not something we want.

Usually, it happens when our Swift Package contains sensitive logic or just private code we don't want the public to know.

Previously in this chapter, we discussed how to solve situations where our packages contain sensitive information and how to create this information and make it one of the package dependencies.

But there are cases when we need our package to be **private**, which could be a problem if we want it to be a dependency.

What Is the Problem Exactly?

The problem is, of course, access control.

When you connect your private dependency to your project, Xcode takes care of the credentials for you. It will probably ask you for a username and password and will save it for later use.

But this approach has two main issues.

First, it doesn't work when your (private) package is a dependency for other packages and not your app.

Second, this method works only on your machine and is based on your private git account.

When working in a team, this could be an issue, and the problem gets even more prominent when we try to implement that in a CI machine.

Fortunately, there are two primary ways to solve that – **personal access token** and **ssh**.

Personal Access Token

Note   The following explanations are based on GitHub because that's the most popular git repository service but are undoubtedly relevant to other git providers as well.

First, I'll start by saying that "personal access token" (let's call it PAT from now on) is **not** the recommended way to give access to private repositories in git, but it's indeed the simplest way.

Implementing PAT contains only two steps:

1.   Generate a new token in git.

2.   Add the token to the package git URL in the
     `Package.swift`.

Generating New Token in Git

To generate a new PAT, we go to GitHub personal menu and choose "Settings" (Figure 6-5).

Figure 6-5. *GitHub personal menu*

From the menu on the left, choose "Developer settings" (Figure 6-6).

Figure 6-6. *Developer settings on GitHub*

And then choose "Personal access tokens" (Figure 6-7).

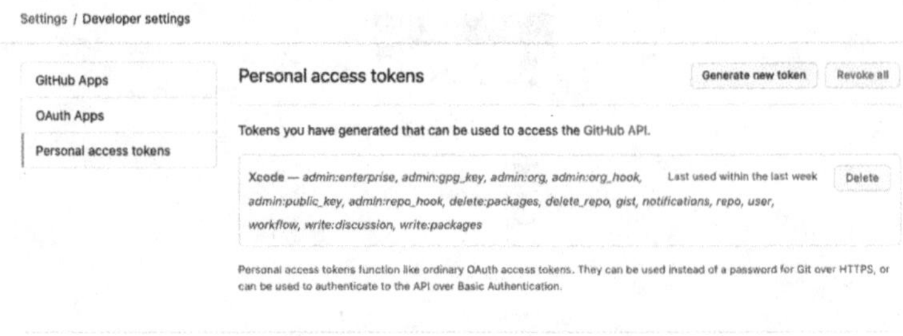

Figure 6-7. "Personal access tokens" menu in GitHub

In Figure 6-7, you can see a button named "Generate new token," which will generate a new token for you to use.

The good thing about PAT is the fact that we can limit the token's access level (see Figure 6-8).

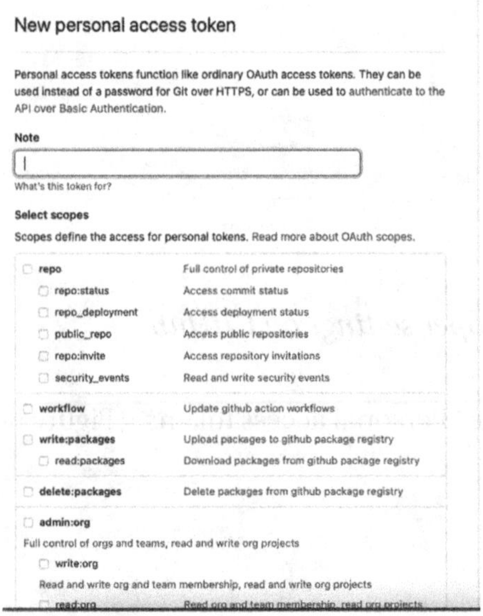

Figure 6-8. Scopes for the token

In the case of Swift Packages, all you need to mark is the first scope ("repo"), and that's all.

After generating the token, you'll see the token itself, and you should copy it to somewhere else because that's the last time it is exposed to you.

Now that we have the token, we can incorporate it in the package dependency URL, as follows:

```
.package(url: "https://<token>:x-oauth-basic@github.
com/<username>/<repository_name>", .branch("main"))
```

This should work for other developers as well and even on CI machine.

The Problem with Personal Access Token

There are some advantages to PAT.

First, as you can see, it's a very simple method to give access without exposing your username and password.

You can always delete your token and generate a new one, and you can also limit what you can do with it by selecting different scopes.

The problem is that a token is de facto, a weakened password. Sure, it is much limited, but it is still a password you expose in your Package.swift file.

Personal tokens are very convenient for personal use or give temporary access to other developers or machines.

To establish a secured connection for other developers and machines, the recommended way is to use an SSH connection.

Using SSH

Using SSH is probably the best-secured method for using private Swift Packages with multiple developers, CI machines, and so on.

Unlike a personal access token, using SSH requires a little more work to set up, but it works flawlessly once you set it up.

What Is SSH Connection?

SSH is a way for a user to authenticate with a server, without using a username and password, but with keys.

SSH contains two keys – public and private. Think of the public key as a "lock" and the private key as the key that opens that lock.

Once we generated the two keys, we put the "lock," a.k.a. public key, on the server and register the private key on the machine, and from that point, we open the "lock" using our private key.

Generating SSH Keys

To generate SSH keys, we need to go to the Terminal and type the following command:

```
ssh-keygen -t ed25519 -C "githubuser@gmail.com"
```

(when githubuser@gmail.com is, of course, your email address).

What the ssh-keygen command does is creating a new pair of keys. The "-t" option defines the type of key we wish to generate.

We can use several other types of keys – dsa, ecsda, and rsa, but ed25519 is considered the most secure and fast kind of key.

The result of this command should look like this:

```
Generating public/private ed25519 key pair.
Enter file in which to save the key (/Users/avitsadok/.ssh/
id_ed25519):
Enter passphrase (empty for no passphrase):
Enter same passphrase again:
Your identification has been saved in /Users/avitsadok/.ssh/
id_ed25519.
Your public key has been saved in /Users/avitsadok/.ssh/id_
ed25519.pub.
The key fingerprint is:
```

```
SHA256:L+sU+XwCXm/fnZSGiY8upXFHP8KyLZCiyIKoZiI/nIM githubuser@
gmail.com
The key's randomart image is:
+--[ED25519 256]--+
|                 |
|                 |
|                 |
|          .   .  |
|         S o o . |
|          o @ =.+oo.|
|oo... . = @.Oo.+.|
|E+=o . . = *ooo.o|
|B.oo  .o oo....o|
+----[SHA256]-----+
```

ssh-keygen will ask you to enter the location where you wish to save the SSH public and private keys while suggesting the default location of saving it in your home folder. You can press enter or provide a different path.

After generating the SSH keys, you need to make sure your ssh-agent is working to proceed. ssh-agent is a system process that is responsible for using the private keys to authenticate with the server.

Type the following line in your Terminal:

```
eval "$(ssh-agent -s)"
```

And you should see this:

```
Agent pid 52540
```

The preceding line means that the ssh-agent works fine, and we can proceed to our next step.

Editing SSH Config File

The next step you need to do is to edit your SSH config file. These files manage the configuration of your SSH keys according to the different servers. This is the place where you configure whether your keys use the built-in macOS keychain, for example.

Create a config file using the nano command:

```
nano ~/.ssh/config
```

And enter the following content:

```
Host *
  AddKeysToAgent yes
  UseKeychain yes
  IdentityFile ~/.ssh/id_ed25519
```

Change the IdentityFile row to the right path if you chose to save the ssh keys in a different path other than the default.

Adding the Keys to the Agent

After adding a config file, we should add the new keys to our ssh-agent:

```
ssh-add -K ~/.ssh/id_ed25519
```

Again, just like in the config file, change the path to the keys' right location in case you provided a different location when generating them.

Adding the Public Key to GitHub

After generating two keys – private and public – we added the private key to our ssh-agent, so it can use it to authenticate with our git server.

What we need to do next is to add the public key to our git server, so it will have "the lock" we talked about.

So, let's go to our package repository in GitHub and select "Settings ➤ Deploy keys" (see Figure 6-9).

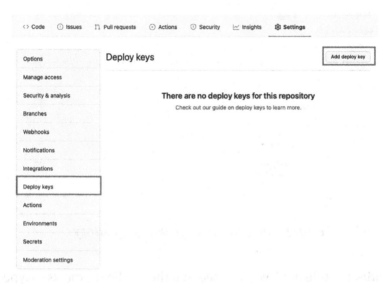

Figure 6-9. *Private repository settings screen*

Tap on Add deploy key, and you'll see two fields – title and key (Figure 6-10).

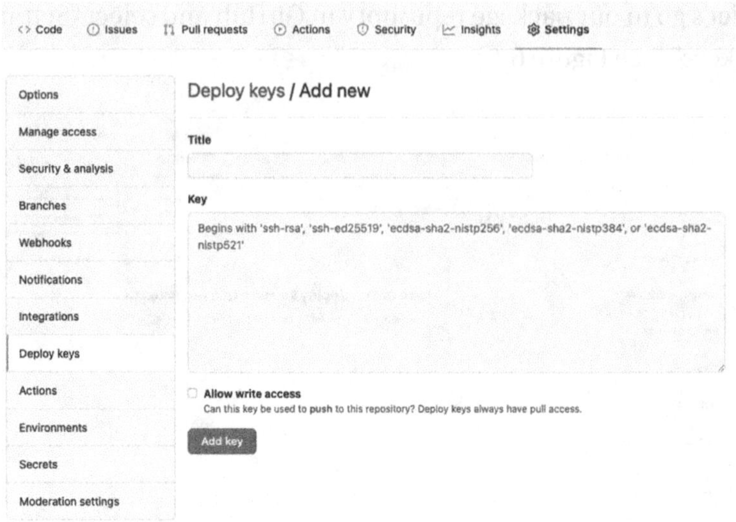

Figure 6-10. *Adding a new key to a private repository*

Besides the title field, you can see that the key field expects to type some text inside. That should be the content of the public key you generated earlier.

To easily copy it, go to the Terminal, and type the following command:

```
pbcopy < ~/.ssh/id_ed25519.pub
```

What pbcopy does is copy the content of the provided file to the system clipboard.

Once you have the public key content in your clipboard, pass it to the key field, and press "Add key."

Going Back to the Package.swift File

Now that everything is set up, we need to go back to the Package.swift file and define our server's dependency.

Just so you won't get confused here, I'm not referring to the `Package.` `swift` file that belongs to the package we just uploaded to git, but to the package that is **trying to use the uploaded package** as a dependency.

In the `Package.swift`, we go to the dependencies section and define the dependency as URL, like this:

```
dependencies: [.package(url: "git@github.com:<username>/<nameO
fPackage>", .branch("main"))],
```

Note that we don't need to add any token or password to the git URL.

To check it, we can go to the Terminal and type

```
swift build
```

And we should see something like this:

```
Fetching git@github.com:<username>/<nameOfPackage>
Removing https://d5864b1121bff4d3c0fc36277f77bccb879cde46:x-
oauth-basic@github.com/<username>/<nameOfPackage>
Cloning git@github.com:<username>/<nameOfPackage>
Resolving git@github.com:<username>/<nameOfPackage> at main
```

Other Machines

Using SSH with git private repositories requires a public key (which is the "lock"), which is supposed to be on the server, and a private key that has to be on the local machine.

This process needs to be done for every machine we want to be authorized with the private repository.

Since the private key is not part of the project, it's a more secured method than personal access token, even though it requires more prework to be done.

The Monorepo Solution

Creating private and public repositories to store a package is an excellent way to share your package code between projects or other developers.

But, as you probably saw, setting up a bunch of repositories and connecting them to your project come with the cost of complexity.

And setting up is just the tip of the ice when speaking about complexity – managing versions between projects, integration tests, and more can become a real pain.

To simplify the process, we can use something called a "Monorepo."

What Is a Monorepo?

You probably heard the term Monorepo here and there.

That's because many big companies use it – Facebook, Google, Uber, and more.

The idea behind Monorepo is that instead of putting each project and each library in a repository of its own, we put them all **in the same repository** (see Figure 6-11).

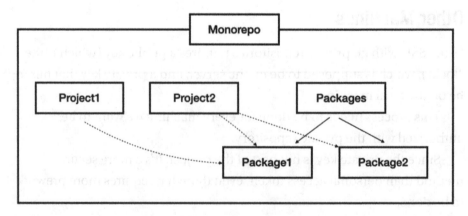

Figure 6-11. *A Monorepo diagram*

While this idea may sound a little bit weird at first, it has several significant advantages.

Dependencies' Management Can Be Simpler

I want to emphasize the phrase "Can Be" because, in many cases and small- and medium-scale repositories, that's the situation.

The fact that all libraries are in the same repository doesn't make dependencies' management unnecessary, but it can make it much simpler.

To understand why, let's see how a Monorepo file structure may look like:

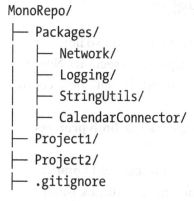

```
MonoRepo/
├── Packages/
│   ├── Network/
│   ├── Logging/
│   ├── StringUtils/
│   ├── CalendarConnector/
├── Project1/
├── Project2/
├── .gitignore
```

The preceding structure is just a suggestion, but you can easily see what we did there.

We created a folder named Packages and put each Swift Package into its folder.

On the same level of the folder Packages, we created the two projects (can be more) side by side.

The Packages folder and the two projects are all inside the Monorepo.

To create dependencies between packages, all we need to do in our Package.swift file is to point to a local package as a dependency.

For example, the Network Package.swift file might contain something like the following:

```
dependencies: [
.package(name: "Logging", path: "../Logging"),
],
```

Looking at the preceding dependency requirement, you see how easy it is to create local dependencies when all the packages are located in the same repository.

Cross-Project Changes Are Easier

Imagine the following scenario – we have two projects and two libraries with a local dependency (just like we saw in the previous section). Now, we want to do an API change in one of the libraries on which both projects are dependent.

The library API changes require us to change code **in both projects** and verify everything works as expected.

Doing that in a polyrepo (a strategy where all projects and libraries have their repository) requires us to clone different repositories, modify the code, push it back, resolve the remote package again, and verify everything is stable.

And to overcome a situation where we push untested code to the main branch or a stable version, we need to check out a branch in the library repository, point the dependency requirement to the new branch, and then merge everything.

You can see the hassle that we have when all we want to do is change a simple API, which was a "simple" scenario.

In the case of Monorepo, this situation is easily handled, with changes being done quickly across all projects and libraries together.

How to Move Forward with Only One Project?

One question often asked when considering a Monorepo is "what to do when we try to branch out and work on a feature in a specific project?"

And that is a pretty good question. With Monorepo, all the projects and libraries are tightly coupled in one repository, and it gives us the feeling that working on a specific branch is awkward.

It is true that when we do a checkout to a new branch, we create a copy of the entire repository.

But code being merged back contains only changes we do, so eventually, most of our commits will be atomic.

Monorepo Also Has Disadvantages

Monorepo can help simplify some issues I mentioned earlier, but on the other hand, it can create other problems as well.

The first issue is perhaps the **git performance and history**. Using a Monorepo means we need to clone all the projects and libraries since they are all in the same repository.

If we have only one or two medium projects, that can be reasonable. But what if we have five or six medium/large projects?

And it doesn't end just with cloning – what about git pull actions when we have a large team?

When we are in a Monorepo workspace, we pull **all the changes from all projects every time**, which can be a large amount of data.

Speaking on git, another issue is **git history**, which is now merged from all projects and libraries.

Another issue Monorepo creates is the inability to **restrict access to certain parts of the code**.

With Monorepo, all the developers have access to all projects and libraries. Again, when we have a big team, this can be a problem.

The last issue with Monorepo – at the beginning of the book, we discussed the impact of having your architecture modular and what does it mean to keep the SoC ("**s**eparation **of c**oncerns").

Using a Monorepo means we are losing the modularity advantages outside the repository.

We cannot share our libraries with projects outside the repository, not to mention making them open source projects.

Solutions to Monorepo Issues

Monorepo is very simple to set up, but as we just saw, it comes with some significant drawbacks, especially when dealing with a big team or many projects.

In the bottom line, like most development issues, it is just a trade-off. And even with Monorepo, we can deal with some of the problems and "pay" with simplicity.

Disassemble Your Monorepo

One option to solve git access, performance, and history is to create several "Monorepos" or a "Libraries Monorepo" (see Figure 6-12).

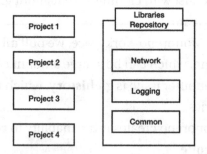

Figure 6-12. *A repository only for packages*

On the one hand, creating a repository only for packages solves the issues I just mentioned but separates the projects from each other.

On the other hand, it makes it harder to make cross-project changes, which is a significant benefit of one big Monorepo.

Changing a library behavior requires us to test the change in other projects.

Summary

In this chapter, we've learned three ways of sharing our code between our projects – a public git repository, a private git repository, and a Monorepo.

Each of them has its pros and cons, and the right way is based on our project's size, security, and more.

Sharing our package increases the need for useful testing, and this is what we deal with in the next chapter.

CHAPTER 7

Testing Is Caring

The trouble with programmers is that you can never tell what a programmer is doing until it's too late.

—Seymour Cray

Emily and the team decided to add a new package to the project. A package that encapsulates text generation logic to share it in the different targets easily.

This package takes a struct as a parameter and returns a generated string based on that structure.

Joshua, the junior iOS developer, was in charge of writing that package.

"Emily, do you have a few minutes for me? I have an issue with the text generation package."

"Sure, what's the problem?" Emily responded.

The issue Joshua has is widespread. Writing a text generator package encapsulates so much logic. It is tough to follow up and make sure we cover all the cases, and things seem to be breaking all the time.

"Doesn't a Swift Package have a tests folder? Just write unit tests!" Emily suggested.

"But I'm not a QA engineer," Joshua was offended.

Kyle heard the conversation and had to interfere: "Unit tests are not for QA engineers. They are for developers to make sure they meet the requirements, and your case sounds exactly like that. Here, let me show you."

© Avi Tsadok 2021
A. Tsadok, *Mastering Swift Package Manager*,
https://doi.org/10.1007/978-1-4842-7049-3_7

Swift Packages and Testing

Kyle was right – testing is a crucial part of development progress. The testing goal is not only to check regressions, but it is also part of the process of checking your code and verifying that it meets the requirements.

Up until now, we've learned how to set up libraries and write code. Now, it's time to make sure our libraries live up to their expectations.

In this chapter, we will learn

- The advantage Swift Packages have with testing

- How to add test targets to our `Package.swift` file

- How to write a new XCTestCase file and provide access to our library's code

- How to write test functions

- How to run tests in different ways – Terminal or Xcode

- What integration tests are and what they mean to Swift Packages

The Importance of Testing

With Swift Packages, testing becomes even more integrated into the process, and that's because of the natural way of building a library.

To understand why, we need to imagine the way we build libraries and packages.

The ways many iOS developers write code are the following:

- They create a method or a function.

- They call this function from a specific point in their project.

- They run their app to that specific point.

- To verify the new function they wrote, developers check the UI, put a breakpoint, or print console messages.

- To check the function with different parameters, developers usually rerun this process and change various parameters.

- Developers need to do the whole (or at least part of the) process if they changed something with the code or fixed a bug.

I'm sure you are familiar with the scenario I just described.

The answer for that burdensome procedure sounds simple: **write tests**.

The problem with writing tests is that it requires us to write a testable code but, more importantly, "move" to the test target (or create one if it's not there), create a new XCTestCase file, and isolate ourselves from the app for a few moments.

In other words, we need to **switch context** just to test something we can do by running our app.

For many developers, the motivation for doing that is ranging from low to not existing.

But when writing a Swift Package, the situation is quite the opposite.

Writing tests is probably the easiest and fastest way to check that your package code works.

Let's open one of our Swift Packages in Xcode and have a look at the project navigator pane (Figure 7-1).

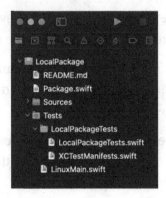

Figure 7-1. *Package test files*

As you can see in Figure 7-1, the package's tests are part of the package itself and are located just next to the Sources folder. While this may sound negligible, it's important since it keeps you in your package development context.

For obvious reasons, our package is testable – it is designed with a straightforward API and is decoupled from the rest of the app.

Also, there is no need to move to another target and rebuild the whole project (only the package itself).

But maybe the most important aspect of building a package is that instead of running your app to see whether your functions work as expected, you just **run your tests**. Sometimes, there is no app at all (in the case of an independent package), and that's the **only way to check your code**.

To summarize, testing a package is a whole different story than testing a function in your project. It's much faster, lighter, and more important – it's just there, so use it.

The Package.swift File

We are already familiar on how the Package.swift looks like; let's look at it again and particularly on the targets section:

```
.target(
    name: "LocalPackage",
    dependencies: []),
.testTarget(
    name: "LocalPackageTests",
    dependencies: ["LocalPackage"]),
]
```

Just like any other targets, test targets have to be declared in the Package.swift file and, of course, need to have their own folder (see Figure 7-2).

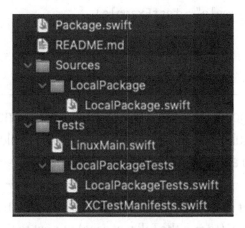

Figure 7-2. *Tests folder in our Swift Package*

As you can see from Figure 7-2, "Regular" targets are located under "Sources," and test targets are located under "Tests."

Our First XCTestCase

Let's open the LocalPackageTests.swift file, which was generated for us:

```swift
import XCTest
@testable import LocalPackage

final class LocalPackageTests: XCTestCase {
    func testExample() {
        // This is an example of a functional test case.
        // Use XCTAssert and related functions to verify your
        tests produce the correct
        // results.
        XCTAssertEqual(LocalPackage().text, "Hello, World!")
    }

    static var allTests = [
        ("testExample", testExample),
    ]
}
```

Note   I'm not going over the whole XCTest framework because that requires a full book to cover, but I'm going to explain the fundamentals in a way that is relevant to our topic.

To run this test case, we need to tap on the diamond button next to the class declaration (to run the full test case) or next to the test method declaration (to run a specific test function); see Figure 7-3.

```
final class LocalPackageTests: XCTestCase {
    func testExample() {
        // This is an example of a functional test case.
        // Use XCTAssert and related functions to verify your tests produce
            the correct
        // results.
        XCTAssertEqual(LocalPackage().text, "Hello, World!")
    }
}
```

Figure 7-3. Run our first test case

Tapping on one of the two diamond buttons complies our package and runs the test(s). Since the test function is empty, our test run ends successfully. Congratulations on your first test run!

Now that we are calm, we can start examining our new test case.

@importable Import

In the LocalPackageTests.swift file, we see many things that help us set up our first test.

The first and perhaps the most critical line is the following one:

@testable import LocalPackage

To understand the difference between import and @testable import, we need to go back and remember what access control is and, by that, realize what @testable attribute tries to solve.

The test target is a different target than the one we try to test; therefore, we need to import it.

However, "import" is not enough to perform a full test.

If you remember, we have several access levels controls:

- public/open, which gives you access to code outside the module

- internal, which provides you with access to code within the module

- private/fileprivate, which gives you access to code from the same class

In general module usage, we only need access to the public methods.

But when running a test, public functions are not enough – we want to test internal methods as well.

And that's what the @testable attribute does – when we prefix an import statement with a @testable attribute, we leverage the access level control "by one level."

This means that internal methods and classes can now be accessed from outside the module as if they were declared public.

What about "private" methods?

After adding the @testable attribute, private methods are now "internal" and cannot be accessed outside the module; therefore, they cannot be tested.

There is a long argument in the testing world if we should or shouldn't test private methods. I'll let that issue for you to decide, but technology-wise, we don't test private methods in XCTest at all.

allTests Variable

Note   The following section is mostly relevant only to Linux OS but can enrich your knowledge about how things work under the hood in the Swift world.

I want to explain what is allTests variable and how it is related to LinuxMain.swift and XCTestManifests.swift files.

XCTest framework uses the Objective-C runtime to retrieve the test methods' list and then run them according to the test runner configuration.

But the Objective-C runtime exists only on Apple operating systems and not on Linux nor Windows.

Since Swift and Swift Package support Linux, we need to find a way to provide the list of the test methods to run.

The allTests static variable contains the test methods' list in the test case and exposes it outside to be managed by Linux systems.

```
static var allTests = [
    ("testExample", testExample),
]
```

If we open the LinuxMain.swift file, we can see how we aggregate the full list of tests from all test cases:

```
import XCTest

import LocalPackageTests

var tests = [XCTestCaseEntry]()
tests += LocalPackageTests.allTests()
XCTMain(tests)
```

If we want to support testing in Linux systems, we need to modify that list whenever we add new tests.

One option to do that is manually adding the new tests to the allTests array.

Manually adding tests is a recipe for failure and defiantly not an elegant solution.

Fortunately, we have a way to do that using the Terminal:

```
swift test --generate-linuxmain
```

What –generate-linuxmain command does is modify the XCTestManifest.swift file and create an extension to the test case with a new computed variable, containing all the test methods:

```
#if !canImport(ObjectiveC)
import XCTest

extension LocalPackageTests {
```

```
    // DO NOT MODIFY: This is autogenerated, use:
    //   `swift test --generate-linuxmain`
    // to regenerate.
    static let __allTests__LocalPackageTests = [
        ("testExample", testExample),
        ("testExample2", testExample2),
    ]
}

public func __allTests() -> [XCTestCaseEntry] {
    return [
        testCase(LocalPackageTests.__allTests__
        LocalPackageTests),
    ]
}
#endif
```

The command also modifies the LinuxMain.swift file by calling the new computed variable:

```
tests += LocalPackageTests.__allTests()
```

Adding this command to your continuous integration flow would be a good idea to maintain these files automatically.

Adding More Test Methods

As I said earlier, I don't want to go over testing methodologies in this chapter. Software testing is a vast subject and can quickly fill a book of its own.

However, there are still some basic rules and principles we need to learn to proceed.

So, let's just make sure we are aligned.

Test Methods Start with "test"

Just like in our example, test methods start with the word "test" followed by a capital letter. Otherwise, they won't be recognized as a test function by the test runner.

Also, a test function cannot have any parameters.

This is an example of a test function:

```
func testNewTestMethod() { ... }
```

The preceding example meets the requirements of a test function. Therefore, it will be recognized and added to the list of tests for the test runner.

Arrange ➤ Act ➤ Assert

Each test is built upon three parts – Arrange, Act, and Assert. This is more a methodologic statement rather than a technical one.

Arrange – The part where we **prepare our data** and bring the test to the point where we can call the tested function.

Act – **Call the tested** function or do the actual action which starts the scenario we want to test.

Assert – Make sure the **results of the action** are according to our requirements.

Working according to Arrange + Act + Assert convention can make writing tests more comfortable, and it also makes them clear and straightforward.

Running Tests

After we added new test functions, our next natural step will be to run them.

There are several ways to run unit tests, each one of them satisfies a different need or workflow, and we'll go over them right now.

First, you need to be aware that in order to run tests, your package needs to compile without errors, and this is also true for any other packages your package depended on.

The good part here is that if your package is part of a project, your project doesn't have to be able to compile successfully, and you can quickly write and test your package regardless of your project state.

To run your tests, you can use the following ways:

- Straight from the code editor

- From the test navigator

- Running the test scheme configuration

- From the Terminal

Straight from the Code Editor

As our first example, running your test directly from the code editor is probably the simplest way to run a test.

Whenever Xcode recognizes a test function (starts with the word "test," etc.), it puts a diamond button next to the function name.

Pressing the diamond button compiles the package and runs the test.

Xcode does the same thing to classes inherited from XCTestCase, and pressing on that diamond button runs the full test case.

One thing to know, though, is that running tests requires us to be on the right scheme.

When you create or add a Swift Package to your project, **a new scheme is created** that helps you configure your package for building, running, testing, profiling, and archiving.

We can have only one active scheme at a time.

Therefore, to run your package unit tests, the active scheme has to contain your package target.

If not, Xcode will suggest you switch your active scheme and run the tests (see Figure 7-4).

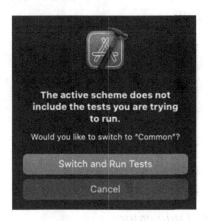

Figure 7-4. *Switch scheme dialog*

Running tests directly from the code editor is useful when working on a specific test function, and we just want to make sure our code is still stable and our test still passes. One example would be a TDD (test-driven development) process when we continuously modify our code after writing unit tests to fulfill different functional requirements.

Once the test passed, the button is switched to a green mark V (see Figure 7-5).

Figure 7-5. *A passed test function*

Running Tests from the Test Navigator

The second place where you can run your tests is through the test navigator (see Figure 7-6).

Figure 7-6. *Xcode test navigator*

By looking at the test navigator (Figure 7-6), we can see that some of the tests are disabled, and some are active.

In this case, the package tests are active, and the project tests are disabled.

This is set according to the currently active scheme configuration, which defines exactly what tests are included in the scheme.

Let's edit the scheme and see how to change that. To edit the current scheme, tap on the scheme name on the Xcode top bar, and select "Edit Scheme…" (see Figure 7-7).

Figure 7-7. *Edit the current scheme*

After selecting "Edit Scheme…," the scheme editor is shown, and we should go to the "Test" configuration (see Figure 7-8).

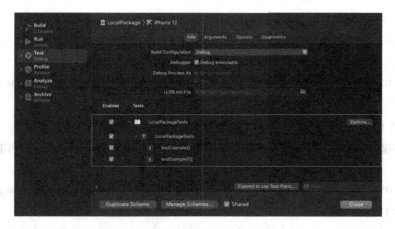

Figure 7-8. *Scheme Test configuration*

Now that's a crucial part of understanding what it means when a package is integrated into a project and how it is related to the scheme's configuration.

We can define exactly what tests will be executed in the scheme configuration window when we run our scheme tests.

To "run our scheme tests," we have two ways:

- Press ⌘ + U.

- Run xcodebuild from the Terminal:

```
xcodebuild \
  -project MyAwesomeApp.xcodeproj \
  -scheme MyAwesomeApp \
  -sdk iphonesimulator \
  -destination 'platform=iOS Simulator,name=iPhone 12,OS=14.3' \
  test
```

Adding/Removing Tests from Our Scheme

The scheme is where we configure our project for each action – build, run, test, profile, and archive.

155

A scheme is required to compile and run a project or a library.

Therefore, when we add or create a new Swift Package, a scheme is being created for you, specifically for that package.

Part of the scheme configuration is the tests' list being run when we choose "Test" from Xcode.

By default, the scheme **contains only tests that are part of the package** or related to the executable if the scheme is built upon the app itself.

However, in many cases, packages are being maintained locally as part of the project you are working on.

In this case, we don't want to run each scheme tests separately but altogether.

To do that, we can press on the plus button, right beneath the tests' list (Figure 7-9).

Figure 7-9. *Adding more tests to the app scheme*

After pressing the plus button, a window with the list of test targets from different modules and extensions appears for you to choose (Figure 7-10).

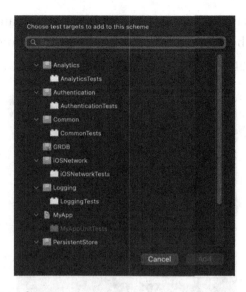

Figure 7-10. *List of test targets to choose from*

After choosing tests from other packages, they are added to the test scheme as part of the project's tests' list.

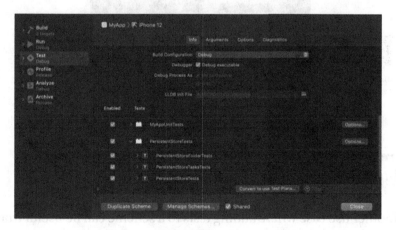

Figure 7-11. *Test Pane, with tests from both the app and the persistent store package*

When we look now on the test navigation pane, we can see that the list of active tests has been updated and includes the tests from the package we just added (Figure 7-12).

Figure 7-12. *Test pane, with tests from both the app and the persistent store package*

Another use case where adding tests to a scheme can be useful would be testing a package **along with its dependencies**.

Think of the following scenario – we have a Monorepo (you should already know what it means by now), and we are doing across change between modules.

We want to make sure these changes do not break anything, so we want to test the **packages' integration** while we are coding.

A convenient solution is to create a list of tests from the package we just modified and packages that rely on that package.

Running this test list makes sure any cross-module changes do not break our app stability.

Running from Terminal

Another way to run tests is using the Terminal. In Chapter 3, I showed the Terminal command `swift test` that can help you test your package straight from the Terminal.

Unlike the `xcodebuild` command, which requires a scheme, `swift test` does not work with a scheme and provides you more flexibility with your test targets.

Running the command without any parameters runs all the tests by default:

```
swift test
[3/3] Linking LocalPackagePackageTests
Test Suite 'All tests' started at 2021-02-13 07:00:29.399
Test Suite 'LocalPackagePackageTests.xctest' started at 2021-
02-13 07:00:29.399
Test Suite 'LocalPackageTests' started at 2021-02-13 07:00:29.400
Test Case '-[LocalPackageTests.LocalPackageTests testPackage1]'
started.
Test Case '-[LocalPackageTests.LocalPackageTests testPackage1]'
passed (0.049 seconds).
Test Case '-[LocalPackageTests.LocalPackageTests testPackage2]'
started.
Test Case '-[LocalPackageTests.LocalPackageTests testPackage2]'
passed (0.000 seconds).
```

```
Test Case '-[LocalPackageTests.LocalPackageTests testPackage3]'
started.
Test Case '-[LocalPackageTests.LocalPackageTests testPackage3]'
passed (0.000 seconds).
Test Case '-[LocalPackageTests.LocalPackageTests testPackage4]'
started.
Test Case '-[LocalPackageTests.LocalPackageTests testPackage4]'
passed (0.000 seconds).
Test Case '-[LocalPackageTests.LocalPackageTests testPackage5]'
started.
Test Case '-[LocalPackageTests.LocalPackageTests testPackage5]'
passed (0.000 seconds).
Test Suite 'LocalPackageTests' passed at 2021-02-13 07:00:29.449.
        Executed 5 tests, with 0 failures (0 unexpected) in
          0.049 (0.050) seconds
Test Suite 'LocalPackagePackageTests.xctest' passed at 2021-02-13
07:00:29.449.
        Executed 5 tests, with 0 failures (0 unexpected) in 0.049
        (0.050) seconds
Test Suite 'All tests' passed at 2021-02-13 07:00:29.449.
        Executed 5 tests, with 0 failures (0 unexpected) in 0.049
        (0.051) seconds
```

But swift test provides more options than that. For example, it can just give you a detailed list of the test functions:

```
swift test -l

LocalPackageTests.LocalPackageTests/testPackage1
LocalPackageTests.LocalPackageTests/testPackage2
LocalPackageTests.LocalPackageTests/testPackage3
LocalPackageTests.LocalPackageTests/testPackage4
LocalPackageTests.LocalPackageTests/testPackage5
```

And we can also filter tests using `--filter`:

```
swift test -l --filter 2
LocalPackageTests.LocalPackageTests/testPackage2
```

`swift test` command provides us additional tools such as running in release configuration, defines if the tests will run in parallel, increases the information displayed while running, and even changes the build folder location.

The `swift test` command is excellent for developers that have to work in the Terminal (e.g., on a remote machine using SSH) or just prefer it over the IDE.

But `swift test` really shines when we want to script our tests and connect them to a continuous integration environment.

Integration Tests

The way we can quickly write tests for packages is incredible. Because our Swift Packages are isolated, writing and compiling them becomes quick and light.

In most cases, tests written inside a package are **unit tests**. Unit tests are responsible for checking a specific part of the code, usually a function or a method.

And while unit tests are essential to maintain a logical code, it is important to check how your packages **work together as a system**. This type of test is called **integration test**, and it's a little bit trickier to set up than unit tests.

Why Are Integration Tests Important?

Libraries are exciting creatures. On the one hand, they are isolated from the rest of the app and agnostic to any app or project we link them.

On the other hand, they are supposed to be integrated with different packages in various projects and perform without unexceptionable.

Setup Integration Tests with Swift Packages

We said that integration tests are all about different layers/modules **working together**.

What does it mean when discussing Swift Packages?

To understand that, we can go back to Chapter 2, where we talked about code organization, services, and business logic.

We said that we have a business layer other than the UI layer (sometimes it is incorporated inside the view model or presenter), and we have services or packages. Take a look at Figure 7-13.

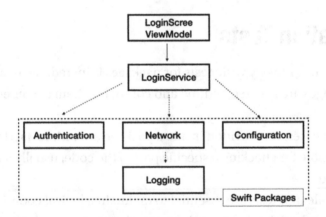

Figure 7-13. *A basic login feature architecture*

By looking at Figure 7-13, we see that we have different packages dealing with different responsibilities. Authentication deals with creating and parsing secured requests, the Network package deals with executing those requests, and the Configuration package handles with saving the data.

Also, the Network package has a Logging package as a dependency.

We want to check here that all these parts I just mentioned work together seamlessly, and the pivot component for that is probably the `LoginService` class.

One way to do that is to test the code inside the `LoginService` that runs when we call the `doLogin()` function.

Another way is to move up in the hierarchy tree and check the `LoginScreenViewModel` to see what happens when the user taps the login button.

Checking the `viewModel` or the `LoginService` is the recommended way of running integration tests. These two classes encapsulate real-world use cases and implement exactly how our packages work together from the user's point of view.

Because our test target imports the app target, there is no need to link the Swift Packages again to the test target, and we can easily set up an integration test as part of the app itself.

But the "Arrange" part is probably the most important one. In integration tests, we need to bring our app to the state when our test is reliable and reflects a real-world situation.

For example, prepare our DB, modify our user defaults, and connect any delegates if needed.

Preparing our app is probably the more complicated part of integration tests.

Link a Package to the Test Target

Sometimes we want to link a package straight to our test target and not rely upon the execution target to provide all the libraries it needs.

One example could be a project where we test different packages and see how they work together.

Another example could be a Swift Package that contains helper tools for testing, and we want to integrate it.

To link a Swift Package to a test target, you need to go to "Build Phases" under your test target settings and add the library you want to integrate (see Figure 7-14).

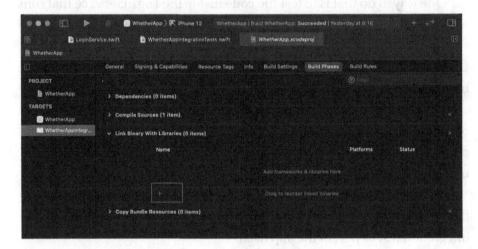

Figure 7-14. *Link a library with your test target*

When you press the plus button marked in Figure 7-14, a list of available libraries appears. This list contains libraries either existing locally in your project or linking to it as a dependency.

Note   Don't forget the difference between a project and a target. In Figure 7-14, we have one project and two targets. We add the Swift Package to the project (locally or remotely), and then we link it to our targets. Test targets are no different in that case.

The problem with this approach is that it is hard to test a real-world scenario run by a specific app or a project, so you should keep it in mind.

Suppose your project is built upon packages and libraries. In that case, your app architecture becomes clear, and a clear architecture is a great helper when trying to set up integration tests, which examine your app very close to real-world scenarios.

Summary

In this chapter, we've learned how to set up test targets, write unit or integration tests, and run them.

Now that we can make sure our Swift Packages run with minimum bugs, we can continue by spicing them up with some resources and assets.

CHAPTER 8

Spicing Up with Resources

Less than 10% of the code has to do with the ostensible purpose of the system; the rest deals with input-output, data validation, data structure maintenance, and other housekeeping.

—Mary Shaw

"Kyle, do you have a few minutes?" Emily asked Kyle. *"I want to unify our login process. The product team wants us to have the same login screen for both of our apps."*

"We already have a Swift Package with the login logic – including network and persistent saving. Isn't that enough already?"

Kyle tried to understand what exactly Emily wanted. He already created a Swift Package that deals with all that.

"I was thinking about adding the UI itself into the package," Emily responded.

"As far as I know, we can't add storyboards or images to a Swift Package. Also, what are we going to do with localization? I understand you're trying to achieve, but I think it's too complicated."

Kyle believed that Swift Package was intended only to contain logic. Adding storyboards, images, and localization looked so unrelated. But things have changed, and now resources can be part of Swift Package.

Kyle's initial thought wasn't that far from the truth – in the first few years, adding resources to Swift Packages wasn't possible.

In Swift Tools version 5.3, Apple fulfilled the long-awaited request and added the capability of including resources such as images, xib files, and other assets in our Swift Packages.

In this chapter, you will learn

- About use cases where adding resources to our package can be useful

- How we add resources

- What bundles are and how we access a specific resource within our code

- How to explicitly add resources and what the differences between process and copy are

- How to localize our resources and even do that with dependency injection

Why Do We Need That?

We said that a Swift Package is a way we can share our code. So why do we need the ability to include assets?

A few chapters ago, we talked about frameworks. Frameworks are actually folders that include code + resources.

"Frameworks" is a tool that we have, that is used to module a full feature, including its logic.

Swift Packages are not there. They are aimed to share and module logical units.

But there are cases where we want to add resources to our Swift Packages to provide more holistic solutions.

Here are some examples:

- A Swift Package that handles the authentication process to service and includes a login screen. It may require a xib/storyboard file and perhaps some images.

- A Swift Package that generates texts and needs to support localization.

- A persistent store Swift Package that is based on Core Data and needs to have a Core Data Model file.

- A Swift Package that can help you share UI components such as buttons and labels. Some of the components require images.

The essence of the preceding use cases is not the resources, but adding them may help you achieve your goal easier.

Swift Tools 5.3

In Chapter 3, we talked about Swift Tools. Just a reminder, Swift Tools versions are the way Apple manages Swift Package features' versioning.

If we want to include resources, our package must support Swift Tools 5.3 and above.

So, we need to make sure your package starts with the following line:

```
// swift-tools-version:5.3
```

And also, make sure you use Xcode 12 and above.

Notice that the Swift Tools version is not related to a minimum iOS version. Even though Swift Tools version 5.3 was released along with iOS 14, you can still use Swift Packages with resources support on previous versions of iOS.

So How Do I Add Resources?

While it may sound weird, in most cases, you just add them. Just drag your resource to your package target folder:

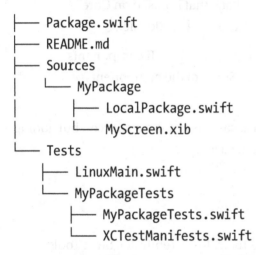

```
├── Package.swift
├── README.md
├── Sources
│   └── MyPackage
│       ├── LocalPackage.swift
│       └── MyScreen.xib
└── Tests
    ├── LinuxMain.swift
    └── MyPackageTests
        ├── MyPackageTests.swift
        └── XCTestManifests.swift
```

As you can see, the MyScreen.xib file is part of the target folder (MyPackage folder), so it can be accessed easily through code (we'll get to that in a few minutes).

But what do I mean by saying "in most cases"?

If we go back to the list of use cases, we see that I mainly talked about implementing screens, creating a persistent store, and handling localization.

And these are the cases where we don't need to do anything special. Swift Package supports certain types of resources out of the box. We can add the following types of resources to our package without making any modifications to our manifest file:

- Storyboards and Xib files

- Asset catalogs

- Core Data files

- Localization files (.lproj)

Other types of files can also be added to your Swift Package, but they require an explicit declaration in the Package.swift file, which we'll talk about later in this chapter.

Bundles

Before we move on, I want to talk about app bundles, which, for some reason, seem to be confusing for many developers.

You are probably aware of the following line of code:

```
Bundle.main
```

And you might have been wondering, "why do we always use main, and what other options do we have?"

Swift Package resources are a perfect opportunity to explain that.

A Bundle, in its most simple meaning, is a folder containing an app or a target resource and executable code.

When you build and run your app, a new bundle is created for you.

The Bundle.main instance is used to access the main app bundle, meaning the main directory of resources.

To access a resource in a bundle, we use the path(forResource:ofType) method:

```
Bundle.main.path(forResource: "data", ofType: "plist")
```

The line returns the full file path.

Does a Swift Package Have a Bundle?

That depends.

The Swift Package code is compiled along with the app itself, and the package compiled code is part of the main bundle.

We can check that very easily.

Let's say that the class WeatherCity is part of a Swift Package, which is linked to the app.

To get the bundle instance based on WeatherCity class, we can use this:

```
let weatherCityBundle = Bundle(for: WeatherCity.self)

// and then check it:
let isMainBundle = (weatherCityBundle == Bundle.main) // true!
```

We see that the WeatherCity class bundle is the same as the main app, even though it is part of a Swift Package.

So, if the Swift Package code is part of the main bundle, what does it mean for resources?

That's part of the changes we have in Swift Tools 5.3.

Once we have resources in our package, a bundle is created during the build and will contain the **package resources only** (without the code, which still belongs to the main bundle).

Notice that a bundle is created **for each package target** that is linked to the app.

Look at Figure 8-1.

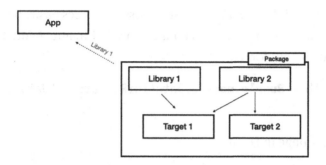

Figure 8-1. *Linking one target only to an app*

In Figure 8-1, we have two targets. "Library 1" contains Target 1, and "Library 2" includes both of the targets.

Only "Library 1" is linked to the app.

So, even though we have two targets (with resources), only one bundle will be created – for Target 1.

Access the Package Bundle from Code

We said that when we add a resource to a package target, we get a dedicated bundle.

Along with the dedicated bundle, we also have a new static variable available – module.

Instead of

```
Bundle.main.path(forResource: "data", ofType: "plist")
```

we need to use

```
Bundle.module.path(forResource: "data", ofType: "plist")
```

The module variable is automatically generated if you have at least one resource in your target folder and won't exist for packages without resources.

With the module variable, we can access resources easily by passing the module parameter to various Foundation, UIKit, and SwiftUI methods.

Generate a path for a file:

```
let filePath = Bundle.module.path(forResource: "data", ofType:
"plist")
```

Load an image in UIKit

```
let image = UIImage(named: "test", in: Bundle.module, with: nil)
```

or in SwiftUI

```
let image = Image("text", bundle: .module)
```

Whenever there is an option to pass the resource bundle, we should use Bundle.module.

Notice that the module static variable is meant to access the resource from the Package itself and not from the main app.

Access Package Resources from the Main App and Vice Versa

So, we know the main app has an easy access to resources using Bundle. main, and the package can access resources using the Bundle.module. But is it possible for the app to access the package resources directly and vice versa?

It is not recommended for a target to access resources located in another target in terms of best practice.

This behavior creates high coupling between your package and the main app and can influence the code-sharing capabilities.

But technically wise, once everything is linked together, all resources are accessible to all targets.

If we want to access a main bundle resource from the package, we can just use this:

```
let filePath = Bundle.main.path(forResource: "data", ofType:
"plist")
```

But, if we want to do the opposite, meaning access a package resources folder from the main app target, things get a little bit more complicated.

The Bundle class doesn't support access to the Swift Package bundle, so we need to provide an interface for the app to allow that.

Here is an example on how to do that in a package. We can add the following variable to our library:

```
public var dataFilePath : String {
return Bundle.module.path(forResource: "data", ofType: "plist")
    }
```

Creating an interface like the preceding example is also recommended when accessing the main bundle assets, but it's a must in this case.

Because all targets have access to all bundles, adding a simple interface is a great way to make use of that.

Explicitly Declare Resources

As I said, interface files, asset catalogs, localization, and Core Data files are all added automatically to the bundle without doing anything special.

But what about other file formats?

Other files can also be added to the package bundle, but we need to declare them explicitly.

To do that, we can use the `resources` parameter in the `Package.swift` manifest file:

```
.target(
name: "MyPackage",
    resources: [.process("logo.svg")]
  )
```

The `resources` parameter contains an array of files we want to add to our package during package linking.

Swift Package Manager doesn't include all resources automatically because, in many cases, developers add files that are not intended to be used within the code, for example, documentation files, code examples, and more.

Adding a Whole Folder of Resources

Swift Package Manager allows you to add a whole folder, including its files.

Instead of adding a long list of files, it is recommended that you just create a resources folder and put all your resources in it.

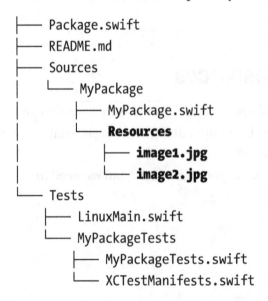

```
├── Package.swift
├── README.md
├── Sources
│   └── MyPackage
│       ├── MyPackage.swift
│       └── Resources
│           ├── image1.jpg
│           └── image2.jpg
└── Tests
    ├── LinuxMain.swift
    └── MyPackageTests
        ├── MyPackageTests.swift
        └── XCTestManifests.swift
```

And on the manifest file size, we can just add the whole folder, easily:

```
.target(
        name: "MyPackage",
    dependencies: [],
        resources: [.process("Resources")]
),
```

Creating a resources folder is recommended not only because it's a fast way to add assets to your package but it's also a more conventional way:

- We don't need to "remember" modifying our resources array in the manifest file every time we add a new asset to the package.

- Once we put all resources in the same folder, we don't care if it's a file that can be automatically processed or not.

- We improve our package organizational structure and make it clearer by separating assets from code.

You might have noticed that I used the process function when I added a folder or a resource. But what does .process precisely mean?

Process vs. Copy

Swift Packages, in their basics, are agnostic to platforms and versions. They can be linked to any supported platform according to what's written in the manifest file.

On the other hand, resources need to be optimized according to the platform and device they are linked to.

When explicitly declaring resources for a Swift Package, we need to decide whether they are being optimized or copy as they are.

To do that, we have two ways to control how we declare files – `.process` and `.copy`.

Let's discuss the differences between them.

We use "process" (or `.process`) if we want the Swift Package Manager to **optimize our assets**, such as images or localization files, when they are being copied to our main bundle.

Using `.process` is the recommended way to copy bundle assets and probably the most common one.

But using `.process` has another effect – it **flattens any folder structure** we put in our target.

For example, let's say our sources folder structure looks like this:

```
├── Target1
│    ├── Target2.swift
│    ├── SVG
│    │    └── files
│    │         └── logo.svg
│    └── View.xib
└── Target2
     ├── Target2.swift
     └── View.xib
```

We want to bundle the SVG folder, so we're going to write

```
.target(
        name: "Target1",
    resources: [.process("SVG")]
        ),
```

After building the app, our bundle file structure will be flat, meaning no SVG and folders at all.

Note   If you are worried about what will happen if we have two resources with identical names on a different folder, you shouldn't. Swift Package Manager doesn't allow two resources with the same name, except for localized variants, which will be discussed later.

There is no meaning for resource file structure in most cases, and it's only for the developer's convenience.

But if we deal with HTML files with images (for example), the internal structure becomes critical.

Using .copy **retains the files' structure** and copies the files as they are, without doing any optimizations:

```
target(
        name: "Target1",
    resources: [.copy("SVG")]
      ),
```

The thumb rule is to use .process over .copy unless you have an excellent reason to do it differently.

Notice we can **process** some of the files and **copy** others. The following example is a good use case:

```
target(
          name: "Target1",
    resources: [.process("files/data.json"), .copy("HTMLSite")]
      ),
```

We **process** the data.json file, which flattens the files' structure, but we want to retain the HTML folder structure, so we **copy** it.

Exclude Resources

Let's take our previous package with the logo.svg file, keep the file in the folder, but remove it from the Package.swift manifest file.

After that, let's run swift build and see what happens:

```
warning: found 1 file(s) which are unhandled; explicitly
declare them as resources or exclude from the target
/Users/avitsadok/Code/ MyPackage /Sources/MyPackage/SVG/files/
logo.svg
```

We've got a warning saying we need to explicitly declare the file or exclude it.

The fact that we added a file to our package doesn't mean we want to add it to our bundle. Here are some examples for files that don't need to be in our bundle:

- Documentation files

- Code examples

- Shell scripts

That's the reason why we need to declare resources explicitly.

But Swift Package Manager demands us to refer **to all resources** located in our target folders.

If it's not a resource that is automatically bundled with our package, we need to either include or exclude it.

Excluding resource is very simple and similar to declaration except that we don't have .process or .copy operators:

```
.target(
    name: "Target1",
    exclude: ["Resources/TODO.md"],
    resources: [.process("Resources")]
),
```

In our code examples, we can add all the Resources folder, except for the TODO.md file, which is a documentation file that doesn't need to be copied to the bundle.

Localization

One of the things that come when adding resources to your package is the need to handle **localization**.

Localization support is built into Swift Package Manager and can be managed easily, similar to what you know from standard iOS development.

To support localization in your Swift Package, the first thing you need to do is to add a property named defaultLocalization.

"defaultLocalization" Property

As mentioned earlier, adding support for localization requires us to add a property named defaultLocalization:

```
let package = Package(
    name: "MyPackage",
    defaultLocalization: "en",
    products: [
```

defaultLocalization property is nil by default, but once we add it to the Package.swift manifest file, we can create localized variants of our resources.

The localized resource variant is chosen according to the current runtime language.

defaultLocalization is used when there is no runtime language or when we don't have a localized resource version for the current runtime language.

By looking at the `Package.swift` interface, we can see that the property type of `defaultLocalization` is `LanguageTag` and not a String.

LangaugeTag is a struct and can be used like this:

```
let package = Package(
    name: "MyPackage",
    defaultLocalization: LanguageTag("en"),
    products: [
```

LanguageTag is used for future expansions, and it has an extension called `ExpressibleByStringLiteral` that lets you pass a String, just like in our first example.

Each time we build a Swift Package, an `info.plist` file is being generated.

Usually `info.plist` files contain the default language value, and in this case, it contains the language provided in the `Package.swift` file:

```
<dict>
        ...
        <key>CFBundleDevelopmentRegion</key>
        <string>fr</string>
...
</dict>
```

It's another way to validate that our localization process is working as it should.

So how do we add different localized variants of our resources?

"lproj" Folders

Previously I said that adding two resources with the same name causes an error and cannot be done, except for localized variants.

Adding localized resources requires us to create the same resource multiple times, one for each language.

To do that, we create a folder with the language code, followed by the lproj extension:

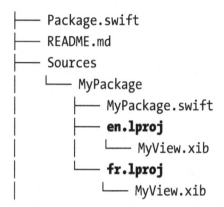

```
├── Package.swift
├── README.md
├── Sources
│   └── MyPackage
│       ├── MyPackage.swift
│       ├── en.lproj
│       │   └── MyView.xib
│       └── fr.lproj
│           └── MyView.xib
```

As you can see, we now have "duplicate" resources. Still, since defaultLocalization is already defined and these resources are located in their language lproj folder, Swift Package Manager is a valid structure.

Whenever Swift Package Manager needs to pick a resource, it does that automatically according to the current runtime language and the matched language folder.

If you are familiar with how localization works in iOS projects, this is not supposed to be new for you.

lproj folders are not meant to include any subfolders, but only a flat list of resources. As a matter of fact, adding a subfolder to a lproj folder will make the package building **process to fail**.

Process

If you remember, we previously talked about the process function. We said that using the process function is the recommended way, and localization is another example of that.

Look at the following package file's structure:

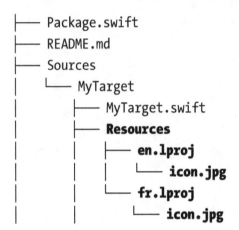

```
├── Package.swift
├── README.md
├── Sources
│     └── MyTarget
│           ├── MyTarget.swift
│           ├── Resources
│           │     ├── en.lproj
│           │     │     └── icon.jpg
│           │     └── fr.lproj
│                         └── icon.jpg
```

icon.jpg is not automatically added to the main bundle. Therefore, we need to declare it as a resource to use explicitly.

But icon.jpg has two variants, located in two folders, so how Swift Package Manager handles that?

The process function makes that easy:

```
.target(
            name: "LocalizedPackage",
     resources: [.process("Resources/icon.jpg")]),
```

According to their language, Swift Package Manager is smart enough to add all the resource variants when using the process function.

Another use of process function is to add a specific resource variant:

```
.target(
          name: "MyTarget",
     dependencies: [],
     resources: [.process("Resources/icon.png", localization:
     Resource.Localization(rawValue: "en"))]),
```

The preceding code will add only the English variant of icon.png.

If we want to add the exact jpg file untouched, we should use copy instead of process and provide the precise full path.

Explicitly Declare Files Outside lproj Folders

Swift Package Manager provides you substantial flexibility with declaring localized resources.

Putting resource files in lproj folders is the easiest and classic way to lay out localized resources in a Swift Package.

Another way to declare localized resources is to declare them explicitly and states the right localization.

To do that, we are going to use the process function again and add the desirable localization symbol:

```
.target(
            name: "MyPackage",
        dependencies: [],
        resources: [.process("img.jpeg", localization: Resource.
        Localization(rawValue: "fr"))]),
```

The preceding code snippet reveals how to add a localization parameter to the process function that will position the explicitly declared resource in the right localized language.

This working method is a substitute for the use of lproj folders.

The localization parameter is **optional**, of course – we haven't seen it in previous examples of process usages.

By default, the value is nil, meaning the process will go under the default language declared in the manifest file.

Provides Localization Texts with Dependency Injection

Adding resources to support localization is a great idea, but as always, in reality, we may encounter challenges.

For example, there are times where our app manages the current runtime language and not the system.

Or we want to use our own localization function to do additional text modifications before we lay out it to the UI.

In these cases, we can always go back to use dependency injection and inject an external localization service from the app itself.

```
public protocol MyPackageLocalizationService {

    func getLocalizedText(forKey key : String)->String
}

public class MyPackage {

    var localizationService : MyPackageLocalizationService

    public init(localizationService :
    MyPackageLocalizationService) {
        self.localizationService = localizationService
    }

    func setupTexts() {
        let cancelText = localizationService.
        getLocalizedText(forKey: "Cancel")
    }
}
```

Using a protocol with getLocalizedText function helps provide any custom localization service that we want.

We can also make this service optional to use and generate even more flexibility for our package consumers.

Once again, we see how protocols can overcome many packages' constraints and decrease code coupling with simple code addition.

Summary

In this chapter, we've learned how to add resources to our package and upgrade them to a new usage level.

We also learned how much Swift Package Manager is flexible and can overcome many challenges, especially around localization files and documentation.

CHAPTER 9

XCFrameworks

> *Just remember: you're not a 'dummy,' no matter what those computer books claim. The real dummies are the people who–though technically expert–couldn't design hardware and software that's usable by normal consumers if their lives depended upon it.*
>
> —Walter Mossberg

Emily gathered her team to discuss with them about a new feature they were supposed to work on.

"Ok, we have a new product, and it's not just a screen. Our server API related to weather information is going public. We need to take some of our code, convert it to a framework, and distribute it!"

"Are they crazy?" Kyle was nervous. "It's our intellectual property!"

"Relax," Emily answered. "It's just the API. It's going to be a binary library anyway; our code is not going to be open-sourced by any means."

Kyle understood, but Joshua still wasn't calm.

"But we have a problem with that," he said. "Our project is based on Swift Packages. We can't just connect a framework to a Swift Package, only to other Swift Packages. It means we need to work with delegates or other design patterns to connect it."

Joshua's concerns were accurate. Up until Xcode 12, we could only use Swift Packages as a dependency to other Swift Packages.

© Avi Tsadok 2021
A. Tsadok, *Mastering Swift Package Manager*,
https://doi.org/10.1007/978-1-4842-7049-3_9

But in Xcode 12, a new welcome feature was added to Swift Package Manager – the ability to connect a binary, XCFramework, as a dependency to a Swift Package. That opens up new possibilities.

In this chapter, you will

- Understand what Swift Package downsides are

- Meet XCFrameworks

- Learn how to create a new XCFramework

- Connect an XCFramework to a Swift Package using both URL and a local path

Swift Package Downsides

We already know that Swift Packages are great. But you probably have noticed some downsides.

The first one is that Swift Package is **open-sourced**. When you link a Swift Package to your app, the compiling process is up to the hosting app.

This isn't always a bad thing, though. It saves you the overhead of building it to different platforms and devices (iOS, simulator, watchOS, macOS, tvOS, etc.).

But on the other side, it may force you to distribute sensitive, intellectual property code.

While this issue might not concern you directly, it may affect you indirectly.

For example, linking your Swift Package to other packages is straightforward, even if they are located on private repositories.

But many third-party libraries are code closed and therefore cannot be distributed as a Swift Package.

This situation pushes them to distribute their code in other alternatives such as CocoaPods or Carthage or, worse, distribute their library as a compiled framework to download when all dependencies' linking is on the developer's responsibility.

Meet XCFrameworks

The fact that Swift Packages are open source has many advantages:

- They are easy to **set up and deploy** – no need to build them for different devices and platforms.

- They are **easy to develop** – it is simple to create a package inside your project and work on it during your app development, with minimum back and forth.

- They are **easy to debug** – when you add a third-party Swift Package and it doesn't work as you expected, you can just dig in the code and understand the problem. Even though searching in other developer code is sometimes a complex task, it's not even possible in the case of a compiled library.

Going back to Xcode 11, other than adding built-in support to Swift Packages, Apple added another natural member to Xcode, and that's **XCFramework**.

XCFramework is a new way to bundle up different variants of the same framework to other platforms and devices.

Not only that, adding XCFramework to a project doesn't require any header search modification or any other setup but simply to drag the XCFramework to the project itself.

On the one hand, we have Swift Package Manager, which is excellent with distributing and managing dependencies. On the other hand, we have XCFrameworks that solve many issues developers have with binary libraries.

The only natural step would be to integrate these two and let developers deploy binary libraries using the Swift Package Manager mechanism.

That's precisely what Apple did in Xcode 12, and it is called binaryTarget.

The arrival of XCFramework provided products such as Firebase (by Google) and AWS (by Amazon) a solution to deploy their libraries as a dependency on Swift Packages.

XCFramework Creation

In a way, XCFramework is a different creature than Swift Package Manager. But the changes in Xcode 12 open up new possibilities for iOS developers to ship binary libraries riding on the Swift Package Manager infrastructure.

To do that, we first need to learn how to create an XCFramework ourselves.

The XCFramework creation requires a little more work than creating a Swift Package, but overall, it is a simple process, where the real challenges are, as always, designing the library API and writing the code itself.

Start a New Project

You don't have to start a new project, but it is recommended and easier to explain the creation process.

Choose File ➤ New ➤ Project, and select the "Framework" template (Figure 9-1).

Figure 9-1. *The Framework template in Xcode*

Give your new Framework a name and save it.

The process of building your framework is similar to writing a package – you can add different targets, including test targets, and you can even add Swift Packages as dependencies (see Figure 9-2).

Figure 9-2. *Adding Swift Package as a dependency to a framework*

193

Also, anything that is related to access levels (public/open, private, etc.) is relevant here as well.

Archive the Framework

The next step would be to **archive the framework**. Archiving means creating the final product to use.

To do that, we are going to use the Terminal:

```
xcodebuild archive \
-scheme MyXCFramework \
-archivePath "../output/MyXCFramework-sim" \
-sdk iphonesimulator \
SKIP_INSTALL=NO \
BUILD_LIBRARY_FOR_DISTRIBUTION=YES
```

Let's go over the xcodebuild command.

The xcodebuild Command

The best thing about using a Terminal for these kinds of actions is that Terminal commands are agnostic to user interface changes, and they are scriptable.

In this case, it is even more prominent because we need to run xcodebuild several times, one for each platform variant.

So, two pieces of advice for you.

First, if you are going to build your framework on a daily basis, it is better to **write a script** for that. Making mistakes is very easy, and in this case, it means that other developers won't be able to use your library.

The second advice is to **read Apple documentation** to understand what options xcodebuild gives you, especially to update you with the latest changes.

Now, let's go over the parameters in the preceding example:

scheme – Write here the name of the scheme you want to build. Remember that a scheme is actually a "configuration to use" when building, testing, or archiving. So, if you have multiple schemes, you should pay attention to what is set in the "archive" configuration.

archivePath – This is where the framework archive is going to be saved, including its file name. It is best practice to write a different location than the framework location itself.

In the preceding example, the archive path is named output, and it should exist before the archive execution, so you should create it in advance.

When creating your framework for the various platforms, don't forget **to change the output file name** each time so that you won't override the existing files.

sdk – Here, you define what platform you compile to. In this example, it's iphonesimulator, so developers (and you) will be able to link your framework while running on a simulator.

If you want to know what the other options are, you can run xcodebuild -showsdks from the Terminal to list the available SDKs:

```
iOS SDKs:
    iOS 14.4                        -sdk iphoneos14.4

iOS Simulator SDKs:
    Simulator - iOS 14.4            -sdk iphonesimulator14.4

macOS SDKs:
    DriverKit 20.2                  -sdk driverkit.macosx20.2
    macOS 11.1                      -sdk macosx11.1

tvOS SDKs:
    tvOS 14.3                       -sdk appletvos14.3
```

```
tvOS Simulator SDKs:
    Simulator - tvOS 14.3                    -sdk appletvsimulator14.3

watchOS SDKs:
    watchOS 7.2                              -sdk watchos7.2

watchOS Simulator SDKs:
    Simulator - watchOS 7.2                    -sdk watchsimulator7.2
```

If you have several SDKs installed for the same platform and want xcodebuild to choose only the latest SDK, write the SDK name without the version itself (like the preceding example with iphonesimulator).

Just like the archivePath parameter, this is another parameter you need to change when archiving for each platform variant.

SKIP_INSTALL – When archiving apps for the App Store, xcodebuild, by default, produces only the main app target. SKIP_INSTALL value is YES, meaning it won't install the other project targets.

But when we want to produce a framework, we should **change that to NO** to have a framework at the end.

BUILD_LIBRARY_FOR_DISTRIBUTION – Should be set to YES. When the BUILD_LIBRARY_FOR_DISTRIBUTION option is set to YES, xcodebuild produces a Swift module interface file that can help your code compile with different Swift versions in the future.

Here is an example of how to run the xcodebuild command for both iPhone and iPhone simulator. I made the changes in bold so that it will be clearer.

```
xcodebuild archive \
-scheme MyXCFramework \
-archivePath "../output/MyXCFramework-sim" \
-sdk iphonesimulator \
SKIP_INSTALL=NO \
BUILD_LIBRARY_FOR_DISTRIBUTION=YES
```

```
xcodebuild archive \
-scheme MyXCFramework \
-archivePath "../output/MyXCFramework-ios" \
-sdk iphoneos \
SKIP_INSTALL=NO \
BUILD_LIBRARY_FOR_DISTRIBUTION=YES
```

The Output

Now it's time to discover what our output folder looks like (Figure 9-3).

Figure 9-3. *Output archives*

We can see that the output folder that we defined earlier now contains two xcarchive files.

xcarchive files are packages (not Swift Packages!), and we can explore what's inside by right-clicking them and select "Show Package Contents."

Each xcarchive content looks something like the following tree:

```
├── Info.plist
├── Products
│   └── Library
│       └── Frameworks
│           └── MyXCFramework.framework
│               ├── Headers
│               │   └── MyXCFramework.h
│
```

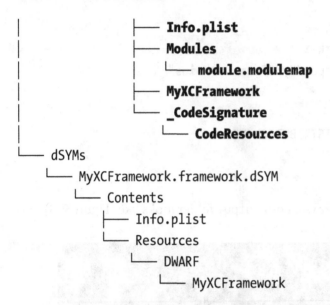

```
|                      ├── Info.plist
|                      ├── Modules
|                      |   └── module.modulemap
|                      ├── MyXCFramework
|                      └── _CodeSignature
|                          └── CodeResources
|
└── dSYMs
    └── MyXCFramework.framework.dSYM
        └── Contents
            ├── Info.plist
            └── Resources
                └── DWARF
                    └── MyXCFramework
```

The framework itself is located under Products ➤ Library ➤ Framework, and it is marked in bold.

What we want to do now is to take all the new frameworks (for the different platforms) we have just created and combine them into one framework – xcframework.

Create XCFramework

Creating the XCFramework from the frameworks we now have is done using xcodebuild (again) with one simple command:

```
xcodebuild -create-xcframework \
-framework "../output/MyXCFramework-sim.xcarchive/Products/
Library/Frameworks/MyXCFramework.framework" \
-framework "../output/MyXCFramework-ios.xcarchive/Products/
Library/Frameworks/MyXCFramework.framework" \
-output "MyXCFramework.xcframework"
```

The `-create-xcframework` command is built from two parts overall – in the first part, we need to pass the list of frameworks we created and, in the second part, the desired location of the generated new `xcframework`.

If everything goes well, we'll see the following message in the Terminal:

```
xcframework successfully written out to: /Users/avitsadok/Code/
MyXCFramework/MyXCFramework.xcframework
```

Congratulations, you just created your first XCFramework!

The Swift Package Connection

XCFrameworks are neat, but the real reason why I'm going over them in this chapter is because of the ability to distribute them using Swift Package Manager.

To demonstrate how to use Swift Package Manager with XCFrameworks, we are going to create a new Swift Package in Xcode:

```
swift package init
```

We don't have to create a new Swift Package to connect XCFramework, and it is possible to do that on the existing package as well, but it is simpler to explain that.

Note   Just like adding resources, connecting XCFramework to a Swift Package requires Swift Tools 5.3 and above, so make sure this is declared at the top of the manifest file. If you don't remember what Swift Tools is, go back to Chapter 3.

What we want to do now is to create a new target based on the XCFramework we made earlier.

Creating a Binary Target

Up until now, there were only two types of targets we used – `target` and `testTarget`.

Now, we have a third type – `binaryTarget`.

Creating a target dedicated to the `XCFramework` we want to add is our way to **connect it to the package**. After we added the target, it behaves just like any other target – creating libraries, tests, dependencies, and more.

Let's see an example:

```
target: [
.target(
        name: "MySwiftPackage",
        dependencies: []),
  .binaryTarget(name: "MyXCFramework",
                    path: "MyXCFramework/MyXCFramework.
                    xcframework"),
      .testTarget(
          name: "MySwiftPackageTests",
          dependencies: ["MySwiftPackage"]),
```

The preceding example shows how simple it is to add a binary target to your package.

There are two ways to connect a binary target – a local path, just like the preceding example, and remotely.

Let's discuss both ways.

Local Path

Placing the XCFramework inside your Swift Package folder is probably the simplest way to integrate it with your package.

There is one constraint, though – it has to be in the root of your package, on the same level as `Package.swift`.

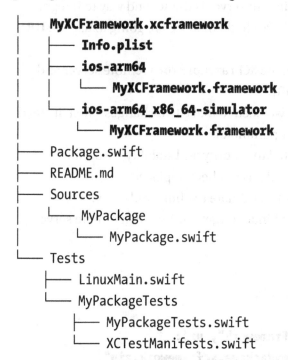

```
├── MyXCFramework.xcframework
│      ├── Info.plist
│      ├── ios-arm64
│      │      └── MyXCFramework.framework
│      └── ios-arm64_x86_64-simulator
│             └── MyXCFramework.framework
├── Package.swift
├── README.md
├── Sources
│      └── MyPackage
│             └── MyPackage.swift
└── Tests
       ├── LinuxMain.swift
       └── MyPackageTests
              ├── MyPackageTests.swift
              └── XCTestManifests.swift
```

As I said, a Swift Package with an XCFramework included is a straightforward method of distributing your package.

On the other hand, XCFrameworks are compiled libraries, which means they can become big, much bigger than a standard Swift Package.

The fact that we are placing such big binaries inside our package can lead to cloning and commit issues because now they are part of the package git repository.

In the case of Swift Packages with big binaries, especially those that you want to share with many developers, it is better to use a different method of integrating your XCFramework, and that's placing it on a different server.

Using URL

Placing XCFramework on a different server is the second way to integrate a binary library with a Swift Package. To do that, we are going to use the **URL** method.

Basically, we need to place the XCFramework on a remote server and point our package to the file URL.

In the Package.swift file, we need to make two changes – first, instead of path, we need to use the url parameter.

The second change is related to security and stability – we want to make sure our binary is valid and has not been replaced.

To do that, we use checksum to validate the binary identity.

Let's see how we connect a binary target, located on a remote server with Package.swift file:

```
.target(
          name: "MyPackage",
     dependencies: []),
.binaryTarget(name: "MyXCFramework", url:
"https://www.example.com/myPackage.xcframework.zip",
checksum: "c246c715ac7f6fae9ef0a89e758a8514644071a164985b1e95d
344a684d84621"),
.testTarget(
          name: "MyPackageTests",
       dependencies: ["MyPackage"]),
```

Looking closely, you probably have noticed that the framework extension is now zip. This is not mandatory, but it's undoubtedly recommended to use.

Now let's talk about the checksum – why is it important?

Unlike the first option, where we included the XCFramework inside the Swift Package, the framework is located on a different server. It means that there is a chance the file **has been replaced with another library** that happens to have the same interface but different implementation.

Other than stability issues, this can also cause security breaches.

What we want to do is to provide some unique identity to the zip file and make sure it is the same file we uploaded.

This unique identity is the checksum value we provide in the `Package.swift` file:

```
checksum: "c246c715ac7f6fae9ef0a89e758a8514644071a164985b1e95d
344a684d84621"
```

To generate file checksum, Swift Package Manager has a Terminal command for that:

```
swift package compute-checksum MyXCFramework.xcframework.zip
```

The resulting code is our `checksum` and should be included in the Swift Package manifest file.

It also means that we need to repeat this step each time we rebuild our `XCFramework`.

Eventually, our Swift Package version is tightly coupled with the `XCFramework` version because of the checksum value.

Summary

In this chapter, we've learned how to create an `XCFramework` and connect it to a Swift Package using various ways.

This capability is the completion of the Swift Package's toolbox because it deals with distributing code in a new way and combining the SPM dependencies' management with the closed code of `XCFramework`.

Index

A

App architecture, redesign
  collaboration, 22
  components,
    relations, 22, 23
  design patterns, 25, 26
  entities
    advantages, 27
    components, 26, 27
    data layer, 26
    definition, 26
  interfaces, 28
  open/closed layers, 24
  paper, 20
  starting side, 23, 24
  UML, 20, 21
Application programming
    interface (API)
  access control
    access level, 63
    fileprivate, 60
    open/public, 61–63
    Private, 59, 60
    uses, 59
  comments
    basics, 75, 76
    code blocks, 78, 79
    discussion, 76

    documentation, 73–75
    document classes/structs/
      enum, 80, 81
    fields, 79, 80
    parameters/returns/throws,
      76, 77
    summary, 76
  create module, 57
  developers code, 57
  naïve developer, 57, 58
  naming
    clarity, 68
    class names, 69
    consistency, 69
    method names, 70–72
    protocol names, 70
  scenario-driven design
    add prefix, 66
    extension method, 66
    flows/use cases, 64
    HTML entities, 64
    inout parameter, 67
    library, 64
    logic function, 65
    stringByRemoving
      HTMLEntities, 66
    String extension, 65
    Swift extensions, 66

Printed in the United States
by Baker & Taylor Publisher Services